Haunted Battlefields
Virginia's Civil War Ghosts

Beth Brown

Schiffer
Publishing Ltd

4880 Lower Valley Road, Atglen, Pennsylvania 19310

Copyright © 2008 by Beth Brown
Library of Congress Control Number:
2008923321

Designed by Stephanie Daugherty
Type set in Burton's Nightmare 2000/
NewBskvll BT

ISBN: 978-0-7643-3057-5
Printed in China

Schiffer Books are available at special discounts or
bulk purchases for sales promotions & premiums.
Special editions, including personalized covers,
corporate imprints, and excerpts can be created
in large quantities for special needs. For more
information contact the publisher:

Published by Schiffer Publishing Ltd.
4880 Lower Valley Road
Atglen, PA 19310
Phone: (610) 593-1777; Fax: (610) 593-2002
E-mail: Info@schifferbooks.com

Please visit our web site catalog at
www.schifferbooks.com

We are always looking for people to write books on
new and related subjects. If you have an idea for a
book, please contact us at the above address.

This book may be purchased from the publisher.
Include $5.00 for shipping. Please try your
bookstore first. You may write for a free catalog.

In Europe, Schiffer books are distributed by:
Bushwood Books
6 Marksbury Ave.
Kew Gardens
Surrey TW9 4JF
England
Phone: 44 (0)208 392-8585
Fax: 44 (0)208 392-9876
E-mail: Info@bushwoodbooks.co.uk
Website: www.bushwoodbooks.co.uk
Free postage in the UK. Europe: air mail at cost.
Try your bookstore first.

Dedication

This book is dedicated to the
believers and the skeptics—
the balance you create keeps
the field of paranormal research
moving in the right direction.

Acknowledgments

I'd like to extend heartfelt thanks to the National Park Service, especially the park rangers with the Richmond Unit, for all of your help and direction.

I am immeasurably grateful to Tim Frederickson and his fellow Civil War re-enactors for their valuable accounts of the happenings on area battlefields after dark.

Special thanks go to my family for putting up with me during the long hours on the road and for helping with investigations.

To the Investigation Team of the Richmond Ghost Trackers—you all work incredibly hard and every bit of your input is appreciated!

Finally, thanks to Beverly Lanier for instilling in me a deep appreciation of grammar, to Joseph Boehling for pushing me to set high standards for myself, and to Anne Vaden for encouraging my quest for answers. You were all very influential whether you realized it or not.

Contents

Author's Note

You can hear the discoveries I made in battlefield audio recordings for yourself and take a closer, full-color look at the photos from the included investigations at:

www.VirginiasMostHaunted.com/battlefields

Investigating the Paranormal

I've been dragging bags full of electronic gear out to allegedly haunted locations for a long time now. Over the years, I've seen lots of investigation trends come and go, promising research blossom and wilt, and many curious people searching for proof of some kind of an afterlife giving up before they have found answers to their questions. The things that seem to persevere, though, are the haunts themselves. The ghost stories and first-hand reports keep coming in, and they are what keep me on my quest for "proof"—irrefutable evidence of the survival of the human essence after death.

The majority of the data I collect on investigations is recorded media, specifically digital photographs and audio recordings. I do not often use the trendy new gadgets and meters that seem to be on every television program about the paranormal, like electromagnetic field (EMF) detectors, unless I am investigating with a team and all of the devices are being video taped. I feel that the best and most solid evidence of paranormal activity is that which I can take home, study in detail, and refer to experts if the situation requires. Experiment with lots of different things and find a combination that works well for you and, if you have them, your teammates.

I like to make notes of "odd" feelings when I'm investigating and I've found that the data collected at those moments often yields surprising results.

Over the years, I've learned to trust those peculiar, almost primal instincts.

Spirit Photography

You'll probably notice throughout this book that I refer to three things as suspect when I find anomalies in photographs: mists, light points, and orbs.

Mists are exactly what they sound like—foggy, shapeless masses that appear in photos but were not seen with the naked eye. I always try and rule out anything that may have caused the effect at the scene, like breath on cool days and nights, smoke, or vehicle exhaust. If you can eliminate those possibilities as the cause of the mist captured in a photo, chances are good that you have something paranormal on your hands.

Light points, a harsh bright spot of light that seems to produce its own glow, is a photo anomaly seen slightly more often than mists. To be sure that you have a true light point, you must first check that there are no reflections of the sun bouncing off of anything in your surroundings.

I've found that taking multiple photos in the same place and in the same position is a good way to narrow down what is environmental light and what is otherwise unexplainable. After you've assessed the lights caused by reflections of the sun, make sure you are not causing the flash of your camera to bounce off of any glass or other highly polished surface. If you're shooting in the daylight, do so without a flash. If you are shooting at night or in dimly lit interiors, try using a flash filter to soften the light and to reduce glare and reflections.

Finally, the most commonly seen and the most commonly debated photo anomaly is the orb. Orbs are rings of light with softly glowing centers that look very much like a bubble. Scientists, photography experts, and seekers of the paranormal all have different theories as to what orbs could be. Some scientists believe that the broad spectrum of light captured by digital cameras, much greater than human eyes can detect, is somehow capturing an image of invisible earth energies similar to magnetic fields.

Photography experts tend to lean towards dust as the main cause of orbs in photos, but cannot explain why orbs appear only *sometimes* in dusty locations.

Paranormal researchers seem to be rather accepting of the idea that spirit energy leaves the human body at death and takes on the most simple of physical forms, the sphere. This theory is usually accompanied by the beliefs that these balls of spirit energy are often moving too fast to be seen with the naked eye and that they only reflect tiny amounts of the light spectrum—those just beyond our naturally visible range.

One thing they all seem to agree on is that none can state that their theory is any more than that—a theory. Personally, I figure I have all of my bases covered with my belief that not all spirits are orbs and not all orbs are spirits. I prefer to examine each on a case-by-case basis and compare each photo containing orbs to other photos taken at the same time and place and encourage you to do the same. A scrutinizing eye is a ghost hunter's best asset.

Audio Recordings

On my search for the paranormal at the battlefields included in this book, you'll find that I often mention I am recording audio data in an attempt to capture something called an EVP. EVP is the shortened name for a startling discovery in the field of paranormal research known as "Electronic Voice Phenomena." Disembodied voices that are unheard by human ears at the time of the recording but are audible during its playback are referred to as EVP.

The recording of messages from the spirit world using electronic devices got its start quite by accident. In 1959, Fredrich Jurgenson of

Sweden made a recording of birds singing in their natural habitat. When he played back the track of bird songs, he heard the voice of a man speaking Norwegian, talking about the sounds of nocturnal birds. Amazed at his discovery, Jurgenson continued making similar recordings and amassed a large number of tracks with disembodied voices over a relatively short period of time.

Jurgenson's collection caught the attention of Latvian psychologist, Konstantin Raudive. Raudive began researching the capture of these mysterious voices in a much more controlled laboratory setting and managed to record over 100,000 messages during his twenty years of work. Raudive published his findings in his 1971 book, *Breakthrough*. He is still today considered the pioneer of EVP research.

So, where are these voices coming from and why can we only hear them when they're recorded? Research, having exhausted every other logical explanation, points to the messages coming from spirits of the dead. It is believed that, while inaudible to the living, spirits are somehow able to manipulate the recording media to create an imprint of their voice or other sounds such as scrapes, knocks, or crashes. Decades of study, however, have yet to determine how exactly spirits are able to achieve this feat.

Well, couldn't you just be picking up pieces of a radio or television broadcast and misinterpreting it to be a message from "the other side?" That is certainly a legitimate assumption, but EVP researchers have found that they can block those broadcast signals, using Faraday Cages and other devices, and still produce the same results. Also consider that the messages received are often a direct response to questions asked by those making the recordings. Can a TV or radio broadcast do that?

Like all aspects of paranormal research, Electronic Voice Phenomena is still a form of evidence that is surrounded by questions and is the topic of much debate. As science and technology have progressed and made recording devices quite inexpensive and easy to use, EVP has been embraced by thousands in search of the paranormal and by those seeking messages of comfort from loved ones who have passed. My feeling is that when we've answered all of the questions we have on the subject of EVP, mankind will likely have already found its "proof" and the quest for confirmation of an afterlife will be over.

Until such a breakthrough in EVP research is made, I encourage those of you hoping to collect evidence for yourselves to consider audio recordings as a possible method of spirit communication. As with photographic evidence, every attempt must be made to ensure that the recorded phenomena are

not caused by "natural" things in the surrounding area. A good rule of thumb is to not allow whispering during your investigations. The majority of EVP are faint and barely audible even with headphones, so loud, clear communication between investigators helps to rule them out as a possible source of the ghostly voices. Also helpful during your review of data is to have everyone present at the investigation record a short sample of their voice for comparison later, should the need arise.

I have found that leaving your recording device alone and away from human interference, known as passive recording, usually results in clearer findings that are easier to pick out from the background noise on an audio track. If the possibility of tampering is an issue for you, try positioning your recorder behind a motion sensor, or, if indoors, you can cover the surrounding surfaces with flour or baby powder to show any traces of movement in the area.

Researching a Haunted Location

Taking all of the various ghost hunting techniques into consideration, I firmly believe that the best foundation for any paranormal investigation is thorough research of the haunted location. History offers us many clues about the possible causes of specific haunts and can help to add weight and credibility to all kinds of strange findings you may come across in the field. Does the site have a tragic past? Was there some other sort of emotional event that occurred there? Not all ghosts linger because of negative things, some may have just been so content with life as it was that they don't feel the need to move on. You can almost always narrow down the source of a haunt doing careful research.

Public records are one of the most helpful places to begin your search. You can often find the names of all of a property's previous owners, sometimes dating back hundreds of years. Try searching those names in your town's newspaper archives or through a local historical society. You may uncover some long-forgotten secrets that could help you determine the "who" and "why" behind a haunted location.

Don't overlook or underestimate the public library as a source of useful clues. While the internet has helped tremendously with some forms of information gathering, not everything on the web is reliable. Chances are good that if you've heard local ghost stories by word of mouth that someone has documented the tale and hopefully done quite a bit of research on the location already. Sometimes the information found in local libraries is all you need to fill in the holes in your background study, but more often than not, it provides only a firm starting point.

Safety

When preparing for a field investigation, remember that your safety and that of your team members should be your top priority. Dressing for the weather and wearing appropriate shoes for navigating all types of terrain fall into the category of safety and must not be overlooked. If possible, bring along a backpack containing a first-aid kit and a few bottles of water. Take my husband's motto and make it yours: "It's always better to have them and not need them, than to need them and not have them."

Another important item that is often forgotten is some means of communication other than a mobile phone. Lots of haunts are in remote areas that may not have cell coverage for miles around. Family radios and long range walkie-talkies are great for communication between team members and can even play a role in signaling possible paranormal activity by making unexplained chirps and beeps. It's happened to my team more than once!

Legality

An aspect of any investigation that should never be ignored is gaining permission from the proper authorities to inspect the property or building. If you are investigating a public place, be sure to do so only during operating hours unless you have *written* permission to do otherwise. Never rely on a verbal agreement to keep you and your teammates out of trouble.

Do not trespass! I cannot stress this point enough. Respect for both public and private property will help you build a good reputation as a paranormal investigator within your community. You will be much more likely to obtain permission to investigate haunted places if you do not have a record for trespassing.

While it may seem like a lot to remember, the steps for thoroughly planning an investigation and collecting strong evidence in the field will become second nature after a little practice. Why not try some ghost hunting in a public place in your town or even a friend's house to get the hang of first? Experience will help you build confidence as an investigator, and the combination of the two will help you open many new doors in your search for the other side.

What Makes These Haunts Special?

- Virginia is the main theatre of battle with the opposing capitals only 100 miles apart. (Haunts are geographically close to one another.)
- The severity of each battle, emotional distress and desperation of combatants, and staggering numbers of lives lost could have left some sort of "imprint" to these relatively undisturbed areas.
- The battlefields were revered as "sacred ground" after the war and were well preserved.
- Virginia has a peculiar geological situation. Is the increase in EMF created by the central fault line to blame for the haunts? Most lie on or very near the line.
- The numbers of paranormal reports that flood in from visitors claiming to have no prior knowledge of a haunt in the area supports their validity.

Are battlefield ghosts the restless spirits of those who were unable to say a final farewell to their nearest loved ones? Do they linger in the fields because their remains were never recovered and given a proper burial? Perhaps these spirits feel so emotionally attached to the places they suffered and perished that the two are eternally linked. I believe that the battlefields of Virginia are home to more than their fair share of each type of haunt.

Take Chancellorsville as an example. The Union army moved in with their heads held high, fully expecting a swift victory. What took place, however, was quite the opposite. The haunts of that area could likely be attributed to a sort of afterlife "shell shock." Those spirits may still, after nearly a century and a half, not fully understand what happened to them.

An example of a haunting caused by lost remains, a spirit that truly cannot rest in peace, could be seen in Petersburg's Battle of the Crater. Many men were killed when a huge cache of black powder was detonated near the Confederates' defensive lines. The amount of earth displaced and the level of confusion at the scene would surely have created an atmosphere so chaotic that many of the dead were simply lost.

A battlefield with a high likelihood of emotional attachment for spirits would be Cold Harbor. Both armies were exhausted, battling in fierce heat and humidity, and feared that even the tiniest of movements would make

one a target for sharpshooters. To compound the miseries each side was already enduring, the order to cease fire and clear the field of the dead and wounded came several days into the engagement. Heavy sniping meant that few dared to venture out of their trenches to assist wounded comrades. Many watched their friends die just yards away, and many more sacrificed their own lives in a feeble attempt to save another. Every aspect of that battle was deplorable and would have undoubtedly left hundreds of restless spirits to walk the fields.

Could geomagnetic forces be fueling haunts in Virginia? Some think so. Most of the major cities in the Commonwealth are built near the largest North-South interstate highway, I-95, which just happens to parallel a relatively small but active fault. In fact, as recently as 2003, an earthquake measuring at 4.3 on the Richter scale shook Richmond.

If you support the idea that entities can somehow "harvest" man-made electrical energy in order to manifest, it would only make sense that they would be able to do the same with energy created by the friction of shifting tectonic plates.

No matter which theory you feel is the strongest, visitors to Virginia's Civil War battlefields all agree that there is *something* at work making each haunt a strong one. The fields all have their own unique manifestations, but the spirits rumored to reside there have so much in common that they tie the locations together and form a "haunted family" of tourist attractions. Join me now as I take you along on my quest to uncover proof of paranormal activity at some of these special Virginia landmarks.

PART ONE

NORTHERN VIRGINIA

Manassas

Beautiful and historic Manassas, Virginia, lies just a few miles southwest of Washington, D.C. Gently rolling hills and sprawling farms make up a landscape fit for a picture postcard. With the exception of a few contemporary roadways and a handful of modern houses, the area remains very much like it did over 100 years ago. It was here in this rural picnic spot near the winding creek called Bull Run that the first official shots of the Civil War were fired on June 21, 1861.

The Union Army was inexperienced and relatively untrained at the time. They were commanded by Brigadier General Irvin McDowell who shared their lack of experience, both as a leader and a hand in battle. McDowell was feeling increasing pressure from politicians to win a quick battlefield victory over the rebel forces to help boost Union sympathies in Washington, D.C.

The Confederate troops were led by Brigadier Generals Joseph E. Johnston and P. G. T. Beauregard. Neither of the Confederate leaders was prepared to back down, even though their units were grossly outnumbered, something the entire Confederate army would grow used to as the war progressed.

Spectators comprised of politicians and the elite from Washington, D.C., made the twenty-five-mile trip with their picnic baskets packed and field glasses in tow, expecting to see a gentlemanly battle ending in the Confederates' surrender. Once cannon fire and rifle volley began plowing through the soldiers in the field, the civilian onlookers removed themselves from the scene with haste. The bloody engagement ended with over 900 young volunteers dead on the hills. Unfortunately, this would not be the last time blood was spilled in such quantity on the battlefield in Manassas.

Just over a year later, in August, 1862, the two forces collided again under the authority of different leaders. The Union army was led by the more experienced Major General John Pope while the Confederates had the advantage of three of the south's strongest strategists: General R. E. Lee, Major General James Longstreet, and Major General Thomas Jackson. Jackson had earned his nickname "Stonewall" at the first battle of Manassas for his fearlessness and was eager to prove himself once again against the incredible numbers of the Union army.

The Confederates took another sweeping victory at the battlefield near Bull Run but not without thousands of men dead. The northern army made its retreat under cover of darkness and traveled back to the protection of the guns surrounding Washington, D.C. The Confederate and Union casualties were nearly equal at around 1,600 men killed per army.

A Visit to the Battlefield

I traveled to the Manassas Battlefield Park and found a spectacular visitor center packed with items that had been retrieved from the field not long after the battles ended. An impressive collection of firearms, uniforms, personal effects, and medical implements captivated me for quite some time. The display rivaled any I had seen so far in the Richmond or Fredericksburg areas. Along with the artifacts, I found a moving series of quotes from men that had survived the engagements and their reactions and shock that came with the first battle on the site. One quote gave a sad comparison of the soldiers' feelings toward the dead in the beginning days of war to their feelings from later battles:

> *"Up on the bluff we saw the first dead Yankee. He lay stark and cold in the death upon the hillside among the trees in the gloom of the gathering twilight. The pale face turned towards us, upon which we looked with feelings mingled with awe and dread… Later on in the war we could look upon the slain on the battlefield with little less feeling than upon the carcass of an animal."*

—Orderly Sergeant William H. Morgan, 11th Virginia

The vivid displays in the visitors' center were rousing in me an uneasy personal connection with the troops that watched their friends fall on these hills. I think that was probably the ultimate goal of the designers of the mini-museum, but I was still a little surprised at the emotion the displays conveyed.

I stepped out the front doors of the visitor center and took in the beautiful landscape. The colors of autumn had just begun to emerge and I could see why this park was so popular with tourists this season. The ridge to my right was flanked with a long, winding line of field artillery standing in front of a colorful backdrop of autumn's changing leaves. Off on the horizon in front of me, I could make out the Stone House used as Pope's headquarters during the second battle and as a field hospital during both the first and second clashes. I headed just a few hundred yards in that direction, to the peak of the nearest knoll, and to the first haunted stop of my visit—Henry Hill.

The Old Stone House was used as a field hospital during both the First and Second Battle of Manassas.

Haunted Henry Hill.

The Woman In White

In the center of the bloodiest portion of the first battle of Manassas was a modest family farm known as the Henry House. Its resident, Mrs. Judith Carter Henry, was the only civilian killed during the engagement when shots were fired at point blank range, striking her inside her home. Her house was reduced to a pile of splinters and rubble as a result of the crisscross of flying shells from the nearby cannon.

The home was eventually rebuilt in 1870, and a later addition was finished in 1883. The building was owned and cared for by the Sons of Confederate Veterans until 1940, when it was donated to the National Park Service.

In front of the reconstructed Henry House is the family cemetery where Judith's body rests with her son and daughter, but where her spirit is said to still walk the grounds in the evening hours.

Late afternoon visitors to the battlefield have reported seeing an old woman in white standing near the graves while they are exiting the park onto nearby Sudley Road. A shaky recording that supposedly captures the elusive woman in white at Henry Hill received very high acclaim on a popular internet video site and is still viewed by hundreds of hopefuls every day. Though personally skeptical, I have still reserved a tiny piece of hope

The Henry House was rebuilt almost ten years after it was destroyed by artillery fire.

The Henry family cemetery is where the "Woman in White" is often seen.

that maybe the person making the recording was just shaking from fear or excitement and the film is genuine. For now, I'll leave that judgment to the viewers rating the video and its contents and I'll set out to try and catch some evidence of the Woman in White for myself.

Ghostly Soldiers on Henry Hill

The Woman in White is not the only ghost believed to roam Henry Hill. Frequent sightings of men in uniform leaning against the huge walnut tree on the edge of the Henry House farmyard have been reported by visitors, Park Rangers, and security staff. The men have been seen at all times of day.

A tourist from Maryland told me that on his last trip to the battlefield, he saw a man under the tree, and his first reaction was that there was a re-enactor just killing time and waiting for visitors to approach the area. When he entered the farmyard, he found no one anywhere around. While Manassas Battlefield Park has frequent reenactments and costumed interpreters onsite for demonstrations, I'm told by rangers that they all stick close to the visitor center and rarely make the uphill trek to the farmhouse.

Could the tourist have seen a spirit that appeared so solid that he mistook him for an actor?

A Monumental Respect

Behind the Henry House stands a monument to fallen troops from the 1861 battle, erected by their comrades in 1865. One visitor and hobby ghost-hunter reported that his hand was touched one afternoon while he was admiring the monument. His hands, crossed behind his back, felt just enough contact to lift a few of his fingers away from the rest. He said he was so shaken by the encounter that he ran to the other side of the house!

Numerous visitors and park employees have caught glimpses of uniformed men standing solemnly at the base of the memorial, only to vanish in a blink or a double-take. Reports of the ghost soldiers paying respects have been made during all times of day, but appear to be highest on the

"In Memory of the Patriots Who Fell at Bull Run, July 21, 1861."

early summer afternoons when Virginia storms seem to roll over the horizon regularly. Many believers attribute this increase in sightings to the anniversary of the battle combined with the free-flowing electricity in the air from the thunder storms.

One of the most compelling stories of paranormal activity at Henry Hill was witnessed by a Park Ranger and a group of visitors he was leading on a tour. It was a hot, windless day. The Ranger was talking about the horrors that the Henry property had seen when he noticed what he said sounded like a child causing a ruckus behind him. He turned to see the cause of the noise and discovered a group of fallen leaves swirling about like a small tornado. Not really knowing how to react, he returned to his tour and the rustling stopped a few moments later. He then claims that his visitors turned very pale and told him of seeing impressions in the grass like footprints as the phantom walked away.

I took dozens of photos on Henry Hill, recorded a few minutes of audio, and a separate video in hopes of capturing some anomalies. I trekked farther along the trail and made my way past an old, sunken farm road that cut through the center of the battlefield. It was between that road and the line of artillery along the ridge that the sounds of men shouting and the thunder of spectral cannon fire had been heard.

I rested for a while at the farm road and recorded a few more minutes of cricket chirps and the rustle of the wind through dry leaves. I moved on to the artillery line for more photographs. When I had collected enough data to satisfy me,

Line of Confederate artillery near the old farm road on the Manassas battlefield.

I returned to my car for a short drive north to the Stone Bridge at Bull Run Creek.

The Stone Bridge

I was a little surprised to find the rebuilt Stone Bridge was just a few yards from the state highway. I pulled into the empty parking

lot and set out on foot to explore the area that has harbored rumors of the supernatural for over 100 years. Sounds of phantom troops marching across the creek at this spot are one of the most commonly

reported phenomenon at Manassas Battlefield Park aside from those reported on Henry Hill.

A popular theory among paranormal researchers is that haunts

somehow derive power from moving bodies of water. Is it the shift in positive and negative ions in the air caused by the water that fuels the supernatural activity? All studies that I have found on the topic are inconclusive. Could it be some kind of earth energy that we have yet to discover or lack the technology to measure that's released by natural bodies of water? For that answer, we'll just have to wait and see.

I walked down to the water's edge and studied the bridge from below. The crossing had been almost completely destroyed during the second battle of Manassas and was repaired soon after. It appeared to be made of two layers—the older, smaller stones near the base and the larger, newer stones making up the arches and road bed.

I noticed that Bull Run creek was more like a small river at this point and stretched about thirty feet across. We were in a serious period of drought when I made my visit and the creek was merely a foot deep at its center. I could see that the water line on the rock that made up the northern bank was well above five feet so I assumed that to be its normal average depth. Understandably, this bridge would have been extremely important to troops with horses pulling cannon and limber to the battlefield a half mile away.

The Stone Bridge over Bull Run Creek.

As I mentioned previously, many researchers believe that running water has some sort of fueling effect on haunts. If the ionic disturbance in the air surrounding a natural body of water combined with emotional impressions left by people during a struggle could cause a paranormal disturbance, the banks of Bull Run Creek would be the perfect place to find one.

I started my audio recorder, in hopes of hearing the phantom march for myself, and sat the device near the edge of the bridge while I took some photos. By that time, there were a couple of joggers and fresh-faced tourists exploring the park, so I gathered my data as inconspicuously as possible. The creek area was gorgeous, even though the drought had reduced the water to a trickle. I took a few minutes to enjoy the setting while the audio recorder was doing its thing.

Sitting on the southeastern edge of the bridge, looking at the twists and turns of Bull Run in the distance, I caught some movement out of the corner of my eye. I glanced to my right, thinking it was a tourist that had somehow managed to come within twenty feet of me on the gravel road without making a sound … and found nothing.

My scalp got that suspicious tingle and the hairs on my arm and neck were starting to rise. It was only four pm and I was really spooking myself. I ignored the uneasy feeling I had and forced myself to shoot more photos in the direction I thought I saw the movement, hoping to capture something unusual. The goose bumps started to subside, so I scooped up my recorder and headed back to the parking lot.

I was more moved by the beauty of the battlefield at Manassas than any other field I have visited. The soft hills dotted with historic homes and patches of old oak and cedar made the landscape look more like something from a Currier & Ives painting than a place of agony and bloodshed. Even if I found no trace of the supernatural in any of my photos or audio files from my trip, I would at least go home with some fabulous memories and impressions of the National Park.

It was a full day before I returned to Richmond to go through the data collected in Manassas. I sat in the dark and silence listening to the audio tracks that gave up nothing more than bird and cricket chirps and the occasional passing car near the Stone Bridge. I was completely disappointed. I felt certain that with all of the talk of supernatural happenings at the battlefield, there would be at least a little something of interest in the audio recordings. Not so. I didn't give up all hope and optimistically decided to scour the photos and see what the outcome was in that area.

Examining the photographs taken at the battlefield was like flipping through a picture book. Each shot of the landscape made me ache to go back and spend more time strolling along the dirt roads that laced through the hills and nearby woods. But I was looking for spirits, not a vacation destination. So I got back to business, scrutinizing every inch of every picture.

The Photos Speak

In one photo of the interior of the new Henry House, I picked up a strange light streak that may or may not have been an effect of shooting through the window. All of the other pictures taken the same way at the same window turned out clean and clear. The second oddity I found was a peculiar blur, almost like a heat ripple, by the Henry family cemetery. This find really struck me because I had seen a strange apparition somewhere else once that looked just like a disturbance in the air—strikingly similar to a heat ripple.

Though I couldn't be sure that the anomaly in my photo was a spirit, I also couldn't be sure that it wasn't. I could find nothing else like it in

The roadbed of the bridge where phantom troops are believed to march.

any of the other pictures, so I was certain that it wasn't a smudge on the lens. I also found no source of heat or anything that might be reflecting heat from the sun in the disturbed area over the grass in the photo. The unusual spot in the image was a mystery to me. Being unable to explain what caused the blur, I filed the shot away as a "maybe" and ranked it a four on my scale to ten of possible proof of the paranormal.

Feeling the rush of an interesting find, I combed through the images taken at the Stone Bridge and surrounding grounds looking for anything unusual. I had hoped for a tiny light or mist, but none presented itself, not even in the shots I fired off when I had the hair-raising sensations. Sometimes it seems that even spirits are a bit camera shy.

Can I conclude, based on my own data collected, that the Manassas Battlefield is occupied by spirits? Maybe. I can, however, take the number and frequency of events reported by those that work on the grounds and the claims of those that visited with supposedly no prior knowledge of paranormal activity and determine that there is a high likelihood of a true haunt. I'm confident that an overnight investigation at Manassas, an idea which the Park Service frowns upon, would produce the sort of evidence that would leave me 100% convinced. Until then, I encourage you to visit the park, enjoy learning about its history, marvel at the beautiful landscape, and take time to note the odd "buzz" in the air around you. You may just catch a glimpse of one of the famous phantoms for yourself!

The Sunken Road

One of the most unusual landmarks of the failed Union attack on Fredericksburg in the winter of 1862 is what is known simply as "The Sunken Road." The road's date of origin is unknown, but historical documents and diaries speak of the thoroughfare as being heavily traveled as early as 1830. The Sunken Road was originally called Telegraph Road and was the major connector from Fredericksburg to Richmond during the Civil War. It earned its nickname from the deep dugout created by the horses, carriages, and wagons that frequented the route. Today the road boasts the title of Fredericksburg's most visited historic site.

To get an impression of how much devastation took place in such a relatively small area, we need to take a moment and step back in time.

Edged by an eighteen-inch thick stone wall, the Sunken Road was a perfect civilian-made trench that allowed Confederate forces to take cover behind the stones and fire downhill on the approaching Union troops. General R. E. Lee could not have hoped for a better position to place his defensive line.

Heavy urban combat took place for nearly three full days in the city of Fredericksburg when the northern army, led then by General Ambrose E. Burnside, made a unified push against Lee's men. The Confederate troops held their ground behind the old stone wall and fiercely defended the Mayre House, a prize of great value to Burnside for its strategic location, at the top of the hill behind them. Union brigades stuck in waves and were slaughtered by rebels in The Sunken Road. It is said that as many as 3,000 Federal soldiers died in one hour.

Despite the heavy casualties, stubbornness drove Burnside to order continued attacks for another full day. By the end of the battle, Lee's men lost 5,300 of their own but inflicted a loss of over 9,000 men on their enemy. It is said that more than two-thirds of the Union casualties fell in front of the stone wall.

The Sunken Road's 600-yard defensive line helped to force the Union army's retreat, but it was a bittersweet victory for General Lee. The north was able to quickly re-supply and replenish their forces and further advance towards the Confederate capital at Richmond.

A dark emotional cloud seemed to hang around that dismal length of roadway for the residents of Fredericksburg and the soldiers on both

sides of the battle for decades. Stories of strange and unexplainable sights and sounds began stirring not long after the fields and road were cleared of the dead. The history of this notorious landmark and its mysterious reputation were too much for me to resist.

Brompton

I visited the Sunken Road with my husband, son, and daughter on a quiet weekday in early October. The tourists had thinned out and the National Park was strangely empty. We split up and I began my exploration near the visitors' center and worked my way towards the heart of the haunt in front of a majestic nineteenth-century mansion called Brompton. The mansion, formerly the Marye House, now serves as the private home of the president of Fredericksburg's Mary Washington College.

Brompton is no stranger to tales of the supernatural. Former residents tell of phantom footsteps walking the halls at night, hearing moans and cries of those wounded in battle who were brought there for care, and catching glimpses of men out of the corner of the eye that vanish when discovered.

Servants who worked at the mansion claim items would go missing only to be found on a different floor or on the opposite end of the house. Some servants were so frightened by the sounds in Brompton, that they fled from their home and employers in the middle of the night.

Unfortunately, the house and grounds are both now closed to the public.

Marye's Heights, now known as Brompton, is currently the residence of the president of Fredericksburg's Mary Washington College.

The site where the Stevens House once stood and where a female apparition has been seen.

A Stop at The Stevens House

On my way towards Brompton, I passed the location of the Stevens House and its family cemetery. The Stevens House itself was gone and its former foundation had been marked with a border of granite slabs by Park Service historians. To the right of the foundation markers was a small stone memorial with the inscription,

> "Here lived Mrs. Martha Stevens, friend of the Confederate soldier. 1861-1865."

A concrete urn covered in moss was the only indicator that a small family cemetery also shared the patch of land with the former house. Claims of a woman seen meandering around the site of the old house and through the unmarked graves have been made by both visitors and neighboring residents.

Could it be Mrs. Stevens keeping watch on her former home? I stopped to snap some photos and sensed a sort of "buzzing" feeling in the air, like I was standing too close to high voltage power lines, but there were no such lines in the area.

The Innis House.

The Innis House

Eventually, I gave up on trying to find a logical explanation for the odd electrical feeling and moved a few yards down the path to the Innis House. The buzzing seemed to follow me like a cloud of gnats. Turning my attention to the Innis House, I learned from the Park Service's historical marker that the modest little building was so riddled with bullets during the battle, that the holes were still clearly visible in the wood walls of the interior.

I realized after I had studied the house for a few minutes that it looked very familiar. It had an ornate wooden trim under the roofline that was very out of place on the simple structure and gave it a sort of gingerbread house appearance. That's when I realized that I had seen the building probably hundreds of times—in the background of arguably the most famous piece of artwork depicting the battle titled simply, "Cobb's and Kershaw's Troops Behind the Stone Wall" by A. C. Redwood. I took dozens of photos, feeling like I had just encountered an inanimate celebrity. I stepped back onto the Sunken Road just ten feet behind me to try and capture some ghostly voices with my audio recorder.

"Cobb's and Kershaw's Troops Behind the Stone Wall."
Library of Congress, Record Number LC-USZ62-134479

The Ghosts Between...

The stretch between the Stevens and Innis houses is clearly visible from the historic homes that border the National Park. Residents there claim to have seen all kinds of unexplained things ranging from mists and soldiers that seemed completely solid, to blue firefly-like "cemetery lights" over the road.

I hadn't heard of any strange sounds being reported in the area, but I was happy to try and communicate with whatever spirits might be willing to talk to me that day. I started the recorder and went through my usual series of probing questions. When I asked if there was any spirit there that wanted to make its presence known, my heart leapt into my throat with the sudden appearance of a white cat that emerged from behind the stone wall to my left.

The cat came from the front yard of Brompton, scaled the wall, and paused for a moment in the Sunken Road to give me an inquisitive look. I watched her for a moment, taking in her ethereal appearance and wondering how she could have made it all the way down the hill in front of Brompton without me spotting her. I had been looking straight in that direction and hadn't noticed a thing until she was on the stone wall.

A few seconds later, she darted down the road to stop and introduce herself to my daughter and receive a few friendly strokes. Then, as cats often do, she jumped up with a twitch and took off towards the residential area bordering the park, leaving just a streak of white. Was she a spirit answering my call or was she simply a neighborhood cat with peculiar timing? I guess the answer to that is in the mind of the observer—I'm still on the fence with my opinion.

An Angel

I wrapped up my recording and moved a little farther down the road to the monument to the Angel of Marye's Heights. This emotion-invoking statue was dedicated to a young South Carolinian named Richard Kirkland for his bravery and compassion during battle. He demonstrated these two qualities by bringing water to his fallen enemies who lay wounded and dying in the field in front of the Sunken Road.

The area around this monument harbors dozens of claims of sightings of a man in uniform, both during the day and at night, along with the disembodied cries and mournful pleas of the dying. I took dozens of photos of the statue and its surroundings and recorded a few minutes of

Monument to the Angel of Marye's Heights, Richard Kirkland.

audio before moving on to the preserved section of stone wall just beyond the memorial.

While the majority of the park's stone walls are recreations, one stretch of the original stands in incredibly well-preserved condition. It was there that numerous claims of disembodied whispers had been heard. Visitors report hearing their names called and mysterious greetings conveyed when there is no one around.

The thought of hearing a whisper in my ear was enough to make the hairs on my neck stand on end, so I recorded a few more minutes of audio in hopes of picking up an EVP. After taking more photos, I continued to the end of the portion of road held by the National Park Service.

The House on Willis Hill

I had completed my trek down the Sunken Road and was heading back towards the visitor center before my walk to the National Cemetery when I passed a closed road on my right with a trail marker. This little turnoff was nearly obscured by the stone wall and the enormous tree trunks surrounding it. It was so well hidden that I had completely missed it the first time I walked by. My curiosity led me

Disembodied whispers have been reported near this stretch of preserved stone wall.

up a steep, twisting trail to the side yard of an empty and disheveled white house on Willis Hill.

It was a strange hodgepodge of additions, some brick and some wooden, that looked more like enclosed porches. I could almost read the generations of change the house had undergone like they were rings of a tree. Curtains still hung at the windows and there appeared to be furniture in some parts of the second story. The yard was so overgrown and forbidding that it took a few minutes of inner debate to figure out that no one lived there.

The small coach house in back of the home, possibly also the former servants' quarters, appeared to be relatively unchanged compared to the main structure. It was a simple square building with a red roof and bubble-filled glass panes in the windows that were clearly over a hundred years old. The vegetation around the small structure was so thick and high that it almost completely obscured my view of the ground floor. Both buildings were absolutely fascinating and I snapped photo after photo there on that hillside.

I rounded the house to what looked like the old back door and took a peek inside through the first floor windows. It looked as though the interior was being renovated or restored and had been abandoned in mid-work many years before. It was then I noticed the buzzing had returned and was much stronger than before. I have been looking for proof of the paranormal for some time now, but I know when to leave well enough alone. Not

The large white house atop Willis Hill was so overgrown that it was difficult to tell if it was occupied.

The disheveled white house as seen from the east.

feeling at all welcome, I photographed the interior through the window and quickly headed towards the Willis family cemetery next door.

The small rectangular cemetery sat in the shadow of the huge ginkgo and magnolia trees that surrounded the house. The path leading to the little graveyard was dotted with wild mint that made each step I took smell of summer juleps. Willis family cemetery was surrounded by a thick red brick wall that was about five feet high. It had a simple iron gate flanked by two enormous white pillars that still showed the scars it earned in the battle of 1862.

According to the National Park Service, the wall and most of the gravestones in the cemetery were completely destroyed by heavy artillery, but the pillars remained. I felt strangely comfortable here compared to my feeling on the grounds of the house just a few yards away. I stayed for a while and admired the view I had from atop a massive tree stump. From that one spot, I was able to see the entire park and a good portion of the town of Fredericksburg.

It was then that the vivid impression of how this hill would have been of great military advantage really sank in. From my position on the old stump I was also given almost a birds' eye view of the National Cemetery that borders the battlefield. I took more photos and enjoyed the panorama provided by my perch a little while longer before making my way back through the gate. My next stop was down the steep path at the Union graves on the neighboring hill.

The pillars flanking the gate at the Willis family cemetery still wear the scars of battle.

The Evidence

I returned home to analyze all of the data I had collected on and around Fredericksburg's Sunken Road. A close inspection found no unexplainable anomalies in my photographs, but I remained hopeful that I might find something interesting in the numerous audio recordings I'd made that day. I pulled out my trusty jumbo headphones and jacked in.

Walking myself back through my visit to the battlefield in the recording, I relived the startling moment I spotted that mysterious white cat and listened intensely for anything that might sound at all unusual. I picked out some strange garbled spots in the playback where I had been standing near the Innis and Stevens Houses. There was the distinct sound of a leaf-blower humming on the grounds of Brompton that conveniently provided me with just the right amount of white noise to make out a faint whisper. I made note of the track and time stamp and continued listening. I heard nothing else but the blowers that had grown from a hum to a full roar when the recording ended.

I moved to the PC to take a closer listen to the strange whisper I had heard over the leaf blowers. I heard myself ask, "Is there anyone here that would like to communicate?" There was the muffled voice I thought

I'd heard earlier. I adjusted the sound levels to reduce the background hiss and bring forward the top frequencies of the recording. I listened intensely and played the segment over and over attempting to make out the quiet message. The human mind will, of course, shape things and contort images and messages to "fill in the blanks" to make sense of a fragment of information. I was hearing the whispered voice on the audio track respond, "Yes. All right."

In my years of collecting EVPs, I have only a handful of times picked up a message that could be considered a direct answer to my question and not just a random word or phrase. The thought of having found one at Fredericksburg's Sunken Road was thrilling. I reviewed the portion of the recording after the whisper much more carefully then, hoping to find another voice attempting to communicate, but concluded this portion of my search with disappointment. My optimism had not been totally squashed, though. I began forging the plans to return to Fredericksburg to attempt a longer, more in-depth recording without the interference of loud lawn equipment.

As with many other haunted sites I have investigated, I found only enough evidence at the Sunken Road to pique my curiosity and make me hungry for more data. All of the things I experienced that day—the white cat with her ghostly timing, the heavy feeling of buzzing electricity with no visible source, and the mysterious voice in the audio recording—were not quite enough for me.

The stories of ghostly sights and sounds that poured from that battlefield so regularly made me eager to make a return visit for more investigating. My instincts told me to be patient and arrange my trip to coincide with the 145th anniversary of the battle on December 13th.

My patience paid off when I checked the Park Service's schedule of events for the week of the anniversary and found that all of the historic houses usually visible only from the exterior would be open to the public. I could barely contain my excitement for the two weeks leading up to the event. Trying to keep busy by digging deeper into research, I was hitting dead end after dead end when it came to the history of the house on Willis Hill.

I wanted to know everything I could about that strange structure that stood ominously over the Sunken Road like an architectural Frankenstein's Monster. I found nothing. My hopes then fell on the National Park Service. My plan was to find a ranger or historical interpreter at the visitors' center who could give me at least some clues that would further my search as soon as I arrived at the battlefield.

As the date grew closer, I started having strange dreams. Obviously, my excitement about the trip had spilled over into my subconscious and the

vivid dreams I was having became an outlet for hidden worries. One dream in particular stood out in my mind above all the others and it focused on the tiny, unimposing Innis House.

I saw myself enter with my husband and take a look around. While photographing a small room on the end of the ground floor, I remember feeling suddenly that I was not alone and that I was certainly not safe. A woman's shrill, angry scream cut through the air and sounded as though it came from an arm's length away. I grabbed my husband and ran outside to the Sunken Road where we stood and watched eerie flashes of blue light dance in the windows and the front door repeatedly open and slam.

I don't at all consider myself any kind of psychic or medium, but I couldn't ignore that kind of frightening detail. This dream about the Innis House had me on edge for a week. It wasn't the events of the dream that had me so shaken up, though. Believe me, I'd love an opportunity to capture a supernatural event like that on film! It was the primal fear I felt in the pit of my stomach before I heard that piercing scream that clung to my conscious and wouldn't let go.

Despite the worried feeling I picked up from the dream, everything else surrounding my return visit went well. More ghostly first-hand accounts at Fredericksburg had been sent to me through my website since my first trip two months earlier. They were more of the same—misty shapes of men were seen near the stone wall, a mysterious old woman was seen at a distance near the Stevens House site and vanished when the witness got closer, and more sounds of battle had been heard near the driveway entrance to Brompton. All of these reports helped to refuel my anticipation. Finally, the day came to load up all of my gear and head for the highway.

A New Trip

The city of Fredericksburg was bustling with tourists and folks in Civil War era costume when I arrived. I knew the anniversary of the battle was a big event, but I completely underestimated the amount of activity that would spill out of the usually quiet town. I parked my car and walked a few blocks down Hanover Street. I traveled through Union encampments in public parks, past a parade of Irish Brigade re-enactors, and around two dozen or so men in Confederate uniforms loading their rifles for a demonstration. If anything could attract the attention of spirits at the Sunken Road today it would surely be this kind of event.

I made my first stop at the visitors' center to chat with the rangers about the mysterious white house beside the Willis Family Cemetery. All they knew is that the house was built right after the war and it was the property of the

Park Service. It had at one time housed an exhibit, but for some reason that no one could tell me, they stopped using the building all together. No offices. No storage. Nothing. Their responses left me with more questions than answers. In a bold outburst, I asked, "Any ghosts up there?"

"Nope, just overgrown hedges," the ranger said. I decided then to hike to the top of the hill and get a closer look before I lost my nerve.

The rambling structure looked even more creepy and desolate than it had on my previous visit. I walked around the grounds and shot lots of photos, much closer than I had before, and captured better shots of the former carriage house. Both the house and garage looked very structurally sound. I stepped up into a screened porch and squinted through the windows to survey the interior—it was striking. Why was the Park Service not utilizing this enormous building? The possibilities swirled around in my mind as I made the steep decent back to the Sunken Road and toward the Innis House.

I waited for my turn to enter the house with a handful of tourists when the dream I had about it the week before intruded my thoughts. It didn't make me nervous or scared, it just put me on a heightened sense of alert.

Before we were escorted inside, the ranger told us a little about the background of the house and how it provided cover for Confederate sharpshooters during the battle. Nearly every surface inside was riddled

The house on Willis Hill had grown even more ragged since my first visit only two months before.

with bullet holes. I learned that the tiny structure had served as a private residence until the late 1970s when it finally became National Park Service property and its restoration began.

When I entered the Innis House, I was quite surprised to find it cozy and comfortable. The original interior walls that divided the first level were tongue and groove boards so battle damaged that sunlight trickled through the wounds from one room into another. The floors were a warm and well-worn pine that sagged just a little toward the center of the room. Recessed lighting had been added to help showcase some of the home's historic features and to provide a soft glow to the rest of the space. The Park Service had "dressed up" the house with fresh pine greenery and white feathers for the anniversary and the overall effect was lovely. Innis House felt much more like a place I'd want to call home than I had expected.

We were given permission by the ranger to explore the first level and I took the opportunity to photograph every corner and detail I could capture. I was particularly drawn to an area under the stairs where a door opened to the outside. It would have been directly facing enemy assault. My attention then was pulled to the fireplace in the central room. The battle took place in a cold, damp December. Did the men take the time to feed the fire and keep their sharpshooters comfortable? My camera clicked away.

I entered the portion of the house that the ranger called the "lean-to," an addition that was built before the battle. It was narrow and dark, but added a small fireplace and about seventy-five square feet to the home where every little bit counted. I was the last one in the building, so I attempted to capture any peculiar sounds I was able on my voice recorder. I didn't ask any questions or speak to the emptiness, I simply switched the device on an tried to feel any differences in the room around me. After about a minute of peace and quiet, with the ranger waiting patiently, I switched it off and exited to allow the next group to enter.

The rest of my time spent in Fredericksburg that day was used to visit tourist attractions and to see the battle re-enactment. The re-enactment was huge, with hundreds of people on the field playing out a shortened version of the battle at the stone wall. It was very moving to watch the actors fall and "die" in the same spots their historical counterparts had fallen over a century ago. During the mock battle, I kept a careful watch over my shoulder for the Angel of Marye's Heights, wondering if he'd make an appearance to help out his fellow soldiers. I saw no misty specter, and if he looked as solid as a live man, I would never be able to pick him out of the sea of men in Civil War uniforms that filled the field.

Bullet holes in the interior walls of the Innis House are a reminder of the intensity of the battle

Battle re-enactment at the Sunken Road.

The Evidence

The festivities died down and I returned to Richmond. After a much-needed night's rest, I began the tedious review of all the data I collected the previous day.

The images captured inside Innis House contained an unusual discovery—tiny lights in the fireplace. They looked like a cluster of tiny orbs, or maybe one that was moving in a circular motion. Either way, it was something that I'd never seen before and I was pretty excited. I examined all of the other photographs from that day and nothing else stood out. Still, I was pretty happy to have found one anomaly out of over a hundred shots, especially one so distinct.

My return visit to Fredericksburg was educational and truly great fun. Can I say that I left with any more proof of paranormal activity than I had on my previous visit? No, not really. I still had the nagging feeling, though, that my timing was just a little "off." First-hand accounts with the Park's ghostly sights and sounds and reports of oddities in photographs came to me so often via word of mouth or web submission that I couldn't comfortably conclude that the Sunken Road was *without* spiritual activity. My only solid conclusion was that I didn't capture the proof for myself.

Fredericksburg's Sunken Road is an emotionally moving place to visit. Walking along the roadway and imagining the battle that took place just behind the dry-stacked stones may be all you need to attract the attention of some of the spirits rumored to reside there.

This group of tiny orbs (in the fireplace) was captured inside the Innis House.

Detail of tiny orbs (in the fireplace).

Fredericksburg National Cemetery

Bordering Fredericksburg National Battlefield Park is the National Military Cemetery of Fredericksburg. Dedicated in 1865, the cemetery is the resting place of over 15,000 men killed in and around the battle at the Sunken Road and during the attempted siege of the city. A plaque at the center of the sea of gravestones conveys the dismal fact that the identities of over 12,000 of the men interred there are unknown.

I have visited dozens of Civil War cemeteries and have found none as remarkable as that of Fredericksburg. I was struck immediately by the carefully terraced levels of the hillside cut to make use of every available square foot of land. Tiny white marble gravestones protruded from each level like rows of perfect teeth. The terrace was topped off by a series of small, rolling hills bordered on three sides by a low brick wall.

What stood out to me most of all as I surveyed the landscape was the incredible size of the trees that shaded nearly every corner of the sprawling graveyard. Nowhere else had I ever before seen cedars and junipers with trunks over four feet wide.

Terracing makes use of the space on the hillsides at Fredericksburg National Cemetery.

Scores of first-hand accounts with the supernatural at Fredericksburg National Cemetery have been submitted to me over the years and most tell of three similar types of encounters—a lone soldier seen standing solemnly near one of the monuments, a man sitting under the trees at the top of the terraced hill, and a crying lady spotted at various places on the grounds.

I have read so many common factors in the stories that I wondered if this could be the solid, easy to confirm haunt that I'd been looking for, or just a viral urban legend. A few members of my investigation team added support to the prospect of the cemetery being a genuine haunt by retrieving chilling voices on audio recordings. One recording captured a peculiar whistle that sounded like someone calling to someone else over a long distance. A different member reported what she said sounded like several rounds of rifle fire in her audio track.

The stories of odd shapes and lights captured in photos from the cemetery were coming in at the rate of at least one per week. The possibility of photographing an entity or hearing a spirit voice in a recording during my visit to the site seemed strong. To say I was eager to begin collecting my own evidence would be a gross understatement.

My exploration of the cemetery began at the top of Willis Hill near the monument to fallen Pennsylvanian volunteers. This spot near the edge of the bluff was reported to be very active and visitors claim to have seen the mysterious phantom soldier here for decades.

Monument to Pennsylvania volunteers that lost their lives at the Sunken Road.

My heart felt heavy for all of the men that were buried there, so far from their homes, and where so much fear and misery was felt during the battle on the Sunken Road below. It seemed like the very opposite of a peaceful resting place to me. With that weight on my mind, I began taking photographs of the monument and its surroundings. Leaning against the enormous granite memorial, I began my audio recording.

I ran through my usual gamut of questions: *Do you want to talk? What is your name? Are you lost or trapped here?* Then I threw in a couple of questions that reflected my thoughts from a few moments earlier: *Are you unhappy being buried here in Virginia? Do you want to go home? How do you feel about so many visitors coming to pay their respects to you and your fallen comrades?* It was about that time my scalp started to react with that distinct tingle and the skin on my arms felt as if I was standing too close to a static-charged balloon. I recorded for another minute or so and snapped a few more photos, hoping all the while that my feelings were right and something might reveal itself. I finally surrendered and moved on to the next monument.

The huge memorial near the center of the cemetery featured a likeness of Brigadier General Andrew Atkinson Humphreys. It was very majestic, but seemed to be surrounded by loneliness. The buzz in the air that I'd felt about fifty yards away at the Pennsylvania Volunteers monument was gone, but I photographed every square inch around the Humphreys monument with anticipation regardless. Again, I recorded a few minutes of audio only without the questions this time. I turned on the recorder, made an announcement to the empty cemetery that I was there to listen if anyone wanted to talk, and waited.

Memorial for Brigadier General Andrew Atkinson Humphreys.

Audio recordings have always frustrated me a little because they need to be analyzed so closely for any abnormalities that it is nearly impossible to tell in the field if you're picking up anything that would prompt longer recording or more human interaction. It is definitely hit or miss. When you hit, though, the adrenaline rush will have you on the edge of your seat and quickly planning your next investigation to record more.

I wrapped up my photos and recording at that spot and meandered through the graves to the top of the terrace on the southeastern edge of the cemetery. I hoped to catch a glimpse of one of the area's most peculiar ghosts, supposedly that of Private William T. Rambusch. Rambusch was a Union survivor of the advances on Marye's Heights in 1862. He watched many of his comrades die in the failed charges and was no doubt left severely traumatized and with a hefty case of survivor's guilt. His discharge from the military for undisclosed reasons a month after the battle at Fredericksburg strongly supported that theory.

Later, Rambusch returned to his native New York, was married, and then left to make his new home in Dodge County, Wisconsin. It seemed to everyone around him then that he had started to make a good recovery.

Mac Wyckoff, a Spotsylvania area historian and editor of the Rappahannock Valley Civil War Roundtable, dug deep into Rambusch's life and published a remarkable article about him in 2004. The article describes Private Rambusch as an honorable and well-liked man in his new home of Dodge County. He became the president of the Bank of Juneau and served until 1896 when he unexpectedly packed his belongings, left his family, and headed back to Fredericksburg, Virginia.

He arrived in Fredericksburg and checked into the Exchange Hotel under a false name. During the days he was traveling, his name surfaced in national newspapers along with the accusation that he had stolen the unbelievable sum of $300,000 from his own bank. A hotel employee claims he saw Rambusch reading an article about the supposed theft in the New York Herald.

Wyckoff then describes two letters written by Rambusch: one to the minister of the Presbyterian Church in Fredericksburg and another to his wife. In his letter to the minister, he requested that his body be buried with his fallen friends in the National Cemetery instead of it being sent back to Wisconsin to be buried by his family.

The story that reads like an episode of *Law & Order* then took an even darker turn. An employee at the cemetery reported that he had seen a man fitting Rambusch's description paying his respects to the dead several times in the few days Rambusch was in Fredericksburg. On October 14, 1896, he saw the man again. When the employee was taking down the flag around five pm, he noticed the man on a bench at the top of the terrace, slumped

Enormous cedar and juniper trees decorate the rolling hills of the cemetery.

against a tree. Further inspection revealed that it was in fact Private William T. Rambusch, dead from a self-inflicted gunshot wound.

Sadly, even though Rambusch qualified for a veteran's burial and had clearly expressed his desire to be buried at Fredericksburg's National Cemetery, there is no record of his burial there. A Fredericksburg newspaper of the period concluded its article about Rambusch by saying,

> *"Why he should have sought this locality to end his life is not known, but one can well imagine the condition of his mind when he contemplated his wrongdoing and it had driven him from home and loved ones, an outcast with naught but a felon's doom in store for him should he choose to live, and however horrible it may have been, it was best that he should die by his own hand."*

Could Rambusch's spirit have felt such desire to be at Fredericksburg National Cemetery that it lingered on? Was Rambusch the man so often seen under the trees at the top of the terrace? I intended to find at least some small clue that would confirm the identity of the spirit and the best way I knew to do that was to hope for communication in an audio recording.

I sat on the bench at the top of the hill and clicked the recorder to life. Using the period newspaper article about the suicide as a guide, I could only assume I was in the right place. I saw no other benches on the bluff, and the trees above me seemed to be the only ones visible from the flagpole below.

"Is there a spirit here willing to communicate?" I asked. After about thirty seconds of silence, I figured I'd cut straight to the point and ask, "Are you William Rambusch?" I waited again to allow time for a reply. "Why did you choose to die here?" The last question sent a chill up my spine. Talking to the dead, even if they aren't talking back, gives quite an eerie feeling. The circumstances surrounding the topic of this conversation weren't doing much to ease my mind, either. It seemed like I'd been sitting there for ten minutes, when I added, "Is there anything else you'd like to say?" Another wait. "Thank you."

I moved about twenty yards north of the bench and took a few more photos. A strange white blur moved in and out of the frame at the lower left corner. I pulled the camera away from my face and inspected the strap, which was firmly around my neck, and the lens cap was held tight by my thumb on the back side of the handgrip.

At that moment, I began to question my sanity and peeked through the viewfinder again. I could see the blur exactly as I had before and was able to snap about four shots before it was gone. In an attempt to explain what I'd experienced, I took some photos at slightly different angles and tried to create a lens flare. I could not make it happen unless I made a quarter-turn to my right. The inability to recreate what I had just seen made my pulse begin to rise with the thought of what I may have captured in the shots. Was something or someone trying to get my attention? Did they hear me using the voice recorder and decide to show themselves?

The anticipation of reviewing the photos and audio started to get to me, so I wrapped up and headed home.

A strange white blur moved in and out of the left side of the frame when I tried to communicate with Private Rambusch.

As usual, I began my analysis of the day's data by carefully inspecting each photo. I combed through each, magnified several times, on my computer. The images that had captured the strange white blur were still just as much a mystery as they had been in the field. Instead of a shapeless mass, the blur seemed to have taken the shape of a sphere or orb and was either incredibly large or incredibly close and neither possibility was very comforting. I found no clues as to the source of the glow.

Still suspecting lens flare as the cause of the light, I forwarded the images to a photographer friend for his opinion about the anomaly. I explained the

optics and design of the camera I used, the position of the sun (which was also evident from the direction in which the shadows of the grave markers pointed,) and the experience I had at the site and being able to see the blur in the digital viewfinder. I also told him how I thought the sun had been playing tricks on me, so I tried to move a few degrees in either direction attempting to recreate the effect but had failed. A few days later he contacted me with his conclusion—it was certainly not a lens flare at that angle, but whatever the cause, he could not explain it as a mistake of the photographer. He said that he thought that it must have been something "environmental" in the frame.

The blur took on a circular shape that was later determined could not be a lens flare.

Riding high on the photographic discoveries at the cemetery, I pulled apart the audio recordings in hopes of finding another anomaly that might support those found in the images, but heard only a few bird calls and the sound of my own voice asking questions to the emptiness.

Sadly, William Rambusch didn't approach me and tap my shoulder at Fredericksburg's National Cemetery that day, but he could very well have been trying to make his presence known in the photos taken near the site of his suicide. The unexplained light in the images provided no clues as to its source or, if in fact it was a spirit, clues about its identity. Still, I had a hard time trying to shake the skeptical view I had of the entire incident because I had no other supporting evidence on which I could rely since my audio revealed nothing out of the ordinary. "Environmental" cause, yes, but natural or supernatural I could not determine.

This site is another where the numbers of reported paranormal occurrences speak volumes. Though I still wanted more evidence to sway my thinking and more time to spend investigating, I know that there will always be a nagging question in my mind—at least until I have that proof in hand: Are there spirits walking the grounds at Fredericksburg National Cemetery? Personally…I think so.

Chancellorsville

Less than eight miles west of Fredericksburg is a stretch of highway called Chancellorsville. Digging into the history of the area led me to the discovery that there never was really a "town" of sorts, but rather the spot on the map was named for the huge home of the Chancellor family that once sat at the intersection of Orange and Plank Roads. The house was a welcome sight for the many travelers that stopped for a meal or lodging and the hospitality of the Chancellors, then operating the home as a tavern.

The brown signs directing travelers to battlefield landmarks and a handful of cannon dotting the landscape are the only things that set this historic area apart from its rural surroundings. I visited Chancellorsville late one afternoon in early October, just as Virginia's busy tourist season was winding down, and the battlefield was a peaceful hideaway in the woods compared to the bustling activity in nearby Fredericksburg.

I'll be the first to admit that when I decided to include the battlefield in this book, I had very little knowledge of what went on there, aside from the handful of ghost stories that were submitted to me and what I had learned from an inscription on a statue on Richmond's Monument Avenue. I was impressed to discover that the history of the battle sounded more like something from the plot of a novel, where the key characters just happen to be in the right place at the right time, than a dry textbook-worthy description that so many rural engagements seem to have.

The Battle

Chancellorsville was a strategic crossroads that the Union hoped to capture during late April and early May, 1863, to cut off the Confederates from the Shenandoah Valley region to the west and their supply lines to the south. When the Federal army became incredibly disorganized soon after their failed attack on Fredericksburg, General Burnside was replaced by his second in command, Major General Joseph Hooker.

Hooker quickly whipped the men back into shape and was eager to make a name for himself. He wanted to be seen as a capable leader by executing a bold maneuver against the enemy. The new commander forged a plan to march his troops through the dense forest known simply as "The Wilderness" instead of using the area roads to move his men. Using the roads would have been the easiest choice for troop movement, but they

would have been quickly spotted by Confederates monitoring the area surrounding Fredericksburg. He hoped to position his forces between General R. E. Lee's men to the south and east and Lee's reinforcements, led by Stonewall Jackson, to the north and west, effectively splitting the Confederate units for an easy defeat. Hooker intended to surprise and outnumber the Confederate troops in the area and force Lee to make his retreat towards Richmond. Though he was successful at outnumbering Lee's troops by nearly two to one, the surprise and retreat Hooker had planned for the opposing General never took place.

The peculiar movement of a mass of blue uniforms through the woodland caught the attention of Confederate scouts, and Fitzhugh Lee, who, a cunning strategist himself, was able to determine Hooker's plan of attack. The young Lee rode quickly to alert Stonewall Jackson of his discovery. The two observed the Union troop movement for less then fifteen minutes before Jackson formed his plan of defense to spoil Hooker's attempt of a sudden strike at the Confederates' center.

Hooker, who fully expected to be the instigator of the surprise attack, was caught off guard and forced to ready his men for defense in the dense wilderness. A fierce battle began and Jackson quickly tightened his men around the Union troops on the western side of the engagement while Lee and his men defended their positions in the southern and eastern portions. The northern army of over 115,000 was surrounded on three sides by a force of only 66,000 Confederates. So far, the only wise move made by General Hooker was to send a unit of soldiers to attempt to break through the Confederate lines at Fredericksburg. He hoped to draw the enemy's attention away from Chancellorsville and to urge them to send a portion of their troops to assist their already reduced defensive line at Fredericksburg. This diversion was enough to aide in the Union army's retreat north.

During his slow retreat, Hooker took command of the Chancellor House and made it his temporary base of operations. Upon discovering Hooker's location, Confederates pummeled the house with field artillery. The house caught fire and the Union forces were captured, killed, or driven out. The Chancellor family was rescued, but their house, or what was left of it after the attack, burned to the ground. The home was rebuilt shortly after the battle but it, too, was lost to fire in 1926. All that remains of the structures today are a few pieces of foundation left to mark the location of the house and a tiny cemetery plot with a few family graves.

The southern troops felt the staggering loss of 14,000 casualties during the battle while the Union suffered nearly 17,000. As the inscription on his statue at Monument Avenue had conveyed, one of the key characters

Former site of the Chancellor House

wounded during the battle was Stonewall Jackson, shot accidentally by his own men. His arm was amputated just below the shoulder and he was thought to make a relatively easy recovery. Lee is said to have sent a message to Jackson during his recovery saying that while Jackson lost his left arm, Lee had lost his right. Jackson, who had allegedly complained of chest pain many days before his injury, died just over one week after the battle from pneumonia while healing from his amputation. Despite the high number of dead and wounded and the resulting loss of his close friend, the Battle of Chancellorsville is said to be General R. E. Lee's greatest victory.

Impressions

The Union army's slow march through the Wilderness was made with optimism. The majority of the soldiers were said to believe that the bold plan of their commander would lead them to victory against their Confederate foe. Instead, their movement was detected and position compromised. Terror swept through their ranks as they realized they were surrounded and that the enemy's counter attack was proving extremely effective. Many fled, but more stayed to fight and face the consequences of battle.

The emotions of the men in the woods likely ran the through the entire spectrum that day. Intense situations, such as those experienced near Chancellorsville, are believed to leave strong psychic impressions. Those impressions, sometimes only lasting days or weeks after an event to

decades or centuries later, are often sensed vividly by the living. A stretch of woods just north and east of Plank Road, near the site of the former Chancellor House, are rumored to hold one such impression.

A Fredericksburg resident and area history enthusiast, Glen, told an unnerving tale of visiting the Chancellorsville battlefield with friends and taking one of the Park Service trails into the woods near the site of the old Chancellor House. It was early summer and the air was already hot and humid as is so common in Virginia. The men noticed, though, a particular stretch of the path they traveled was unusually cold. They were attempting an exchange of logical explanations for the cold area when they heard a low moan and calls for help from about twenty feet away. They searched everywhere around them, thinking that there may have been an injured jogger or someone else that had fallen, but turned up nothing. There was no place for anyone to hide and the men could find no source for the sound they had just heard.

Glen said that it was about that time they put two and two together and fled the woods. Interestingly, I discovered a few reports of men in uniform seen in those same woods by drivers on Plank Road. All those that submitted reports claim to have seen the men in either a quick glance towards the trees or out of the corner of their eye. A second look revealed nothing but wilderness.

Another of Chancellorsville's "hot spots" is the area of Confederate trenches near the park's driving tour road that runs through the heart of the battlefield. Sightings of men in the woods and laying, with weapons at the ready, in the trenches there have been reported by visitors and park

Apparitions of Confederate soldiers have been reported in the trenches near Ranger Lane.

employees alike. A former resident of Ranger Lane also claims to have heard the sounds of men shouting and rifle fire many times in the very early hours of the morning. He said that one night, the sounds were so close and so loud that he was awakened from a deep sleep and ran outside expecting to find a group of trespassers or fellow rangers playing a prank. There was no one in sight and all of the other area residents adamantly denied participating in any sort of practical joke.

One of my favorite tales of ghosts from Chancellorsville involves a resident of Fredericksburg on her way home and needing to stop for an emergency bathroom break. She's a government employee hoping to preserve anonymity, so let's just call her Judy.

She felt she couldn't make it the five or six miles to the nearest service station and decided to have her husband pull over on Orange Road near the Plank Road intersection. To avoid the gaze of passing motorists, Judy hurried into the woods about twenty yards and found a depression in the ground that made the perfect out-of-sight place to stop. Taking care of business, she noticed a couple of small campfires deeper in the woods and decided to hurry along before attracting attention. A cold and heavy hand then touched her shoulder and she heard a voice from behind her say, "Ma'am, you shouldn't be back here."

Startled that anyone could have tiptoed up to her without being heard, she spun around and found no one. Judy claims that it was years after this spooky experience that she learned the patch of woods in which she had chosen to relieve herself was one of the same that Union troops had moved though in an attempt to surprise the Confederates. There was no doubt in her mind then as to what she had witnessed.

I took the driving tour through the park just before dusk and made a special stop at the trenches where the sightings had been

The only marked grave at the Chancellor site is that belonging to two infants who died in the early twentieth century.

reported. After taking a few photos in hopes of catching a glimpse of one of the elusive specters, I followed the narrow road, keeping a careful eye out for deer that time of day, towards the most well-known and well-seen stop on my visit.

The grounds where the original and reconstructed Chancellor Houses stood, less than two hundred yards from the area where Glen and his friends had their chilling experience in the woods, have had their own fair share of reported phenomena. Clearly visible from the two intersecting roads, the tiny family graveyard and its "cemetery lights" have caught the attention of many

drivers stopped at the neighboring traffic signal. The lights are most often described as two hazy blue fireflies that dart around just a few feet above the grass.

I made a stop by the Chancellor House foundation markers and the family cemetery just before sundown. I was only able to snap a handful of photographs before rangers came by to alert me of the park's closing time. Instead of grilling the rangers about the rumors of ghosts at Chancellorsville, already knowing that most Park Service employees don't give up any kind of confirmation of paranormal activity without a struggle, I left as instructed.

I returned home from my tour of Northern Virginia battlefields a few days after my trip to Chancellorsville and I was eager to review the photos I had taken that day. I retraced my driving tour in the numerous photos shot from my car window and made my way to the infamous Confederate trenches. Every photo was crystal clear, surprising for the late hour in which they were taken, and revealed no ghostly faces or light anomalies.

I clicked through and examined the images of the family graveyard and the bricks marking the former location of the Chancellor House only to discover that each was mysteriously fuzzy. Out of fourteen photographs of the site, I was able to make out details in only two of them. Unfortunately, those two didn't give up any evidence of paranormal

All that remains of the historic Chancellor home is a crumbling set of steps.

activity. I have no explanation for the hazy images that were taken at that pull-off near the historic crossroads. The photos preceding the blurred set were taken under the same circumstances with no adverse results, likewise for those that were taken after. I made no note of having to stop and clean the camera lens. I was skeptical at first, which is my nature, but starting to change my mind when I found a lot of folks that were quick to chalk it up to supernatural interference.

The number of tales swirling around the battlefield of unexplainable sights and sounds, still intrigue me. I've held onto my blurry photos just in case I can learn more from them in the future, perhaps after some remarkable breakthrough in paranormal research. They're my souvenir of my visit to the battlefield in the wilderness and one thing I can say I took home that day that was truly unusual.

PART TWO

RICHMOND

Belle Island

Belle Isle is the largest of the islands in the James River in downtown Richmond at just over fifty acres in size. From May through August, the rocky little piece of land is like a lush river resort isolated from the bustling city by the James' churning rapids. Virginia's humid summers draw people from the surrounding city and its neighboring counties to make the trek across the swaying pedestrian bridge for picnics or a swim in the shallows. Aside from a handful of site markers donated by the Sierra Club and a couple of small stone ruins, the island's present beauty gives few clues of the horrors its residents endured during the Civil War. The historical research I conducted before my visit to the island revealed a past so grisly that I began having second thoughts about conducting an investigation there.

A Prison

Belle Island was used as a prison camp for enlisted Union soldiers from 1862 until Richmond's evacuation in 1865. In that relatively short span, the island earned a miserable reputation like that of the notorious facility at Andersonville, Georgia. The prison population fluctuated from extreme overcrowding to just a few hundred men or less held at a time. The island was closed several times when a particularly large prisoner exchange was made between the Union and the Confederacy that emptied its roster.

No barracks were ever erected on the site—men were instead kept in tents or in the open air when the island more than doubled its limit of 3,000 prisoners. During the three years Belle Isle served as a prison, it is estimated that thousands of men died there from starvation, dysentery, bullets from the guards' rifles, or exposure. Records of the period show that the more slow and agonizing deaths claimed the majority.

Of all of the places in and around Richmond that harbor rumors of paranormal events, no other has the wide variety of phenomena reported like Belle Isle. I certainly can't argue that the island saw more than its share of physical pain and emotional torture.

I've been told by several hikers making their way around the island trail that they heard the distinct sounds of footsteps on the path behind them. All claimed to look and find no one there. Reports made by dozens of visitors to the island involve them being hit with small stones, thrown from unseen hands, near the ruins of a hydroelectric plant on the south

bank. The two most common tales from Belle Island are of mysterious whispers and anomalous photos. Both of these phenomena seem to occur at equal frequency to visitors that claim to have had no prior knowledge of paranormal activity there and to those that visit the island searching for ghosts.

A friend and local occult researcher, Ash, went to Belle Island with a few others seeking proof of supernatural activity, by attempting to communicate with spirits using a pendulum. Ash is quite proficient with the technique and has had a level of success in blind tests. He told me of how he made contact with a few spirits that were somehow bound to the island and were curious about their situation. He had answered some of their questions and asked more of his own when he suddenly experienced strong negative movements with the pendulum. Whatever the force was, it severed the communication with the other spirits and its strength disturbed Ash and his team so much, that they immediately left the island. He says that the pendulum he used that day, even after repeated cleansings, has not since given him any positive response.

Tad Hill is another friend and paranormal investigator that told me of his several encounters with the spirits at Belle Isle. Tad lives just a few miles from the island and makes regular hikes there. On more than one occasion he has heard the mysterious footsteps behind him on one particularly dark stretch of trail. Once, he whipped around and snapped a picture after hearing the crunching of phantom feet. The photo captured an orb-like anomaly in the middle of the day and without using a flash. This odd photograph is one of many that he has collected from all parts of the island.

I had been told so many stories of first-hand experiences with the paranormal at Belle Island from friends, colleagues, and strangers over the years that I arranged to take a team of about twenty investigators there on a training trip. I figured that if I had folks on the team that still needed to see proof with their own eyes before they could forge a firm belief in ghosts, they would definitely find it on that dismal island.

We assembled two crews, each with a goal of collecting still photos, audio, and video in hopes of capturing evidence of the supernatural activity there. While the subjects of spirit photography and electronic voice phenomena (EVP) are still hotly debated by both believers and skeptics alike, I have found that they earn a bit more credibility when collected simultaneously.

We ventured across the river on a Sunday evening not long after Labor Day. The weather was crisp and clear with the approach of Autumn. The perfect hiking weather made the trip worthwhile even if we didn't come away with the evidence we hoped. The James River Park System and the

City of Richmond Police Department were combating a long-term problem with vandals and the homeless setting fires on the island at night, so they were enforcing a strict daylight-only policy for the park.

A few of the team expressed their disappointment but held on to their optimism—the number of daytime reports was nearly that of nighttime. I held back on telling them any of the details that I had learned from witnesses about their experiences for fear of tainting the investigators' perceptions, and instructed the team members who had visited the island in

the past to keep quiet as well. I instead relayed the type of events reported (sounds, apparitions, shadow people, moving objects, and strange lights in photos) and the most concentrated areas of paranormal claims on the small island. I sent them on their way.

I stayed with the group more focused on capturing photo anomalies, but readied my digital voice recorder to appease my own curiosity. We went to the area just off of the bridge that was Belle Island's main burial ground and started snapping shots. Hundreds, if not thousands, of men were interred at

that site at varying depths to make best use of the small patch of land. As with most of the crowded gravesites from this wartime, many of the identities of the soldiers and records of the number of men buried there were either lost or never documented. I kept my recorder in one hand while I took a few photos of the team at work. We gathered data at that site for about ten minutes and then moved west along the trail at the river's edge.

This low and rocky portion of the island was where the highest concentration of tents was located and where hundreds of prisoners froze to death during the night. We walked in and out of several cold spots and snapped photos of the surrounding woods while the sun dipped towards the horizon. The shadows had grown long and we were all starting to feel a little uneasy about our investigation.

Our next stop was the ruin of the early twentieth-century hydroelectric plant on the south bank. The darkness on that side of the island was much more than we had anticipated and the lack of light seemed to intensify the negativity in the air around us. I understood then why the majority of the stories involving

The small cemetery area on the north bank of Belle Island.

Ruins of the hydroelectric plant on the "dark side" of Belle Isle are rumored to house malevolent spirits.

malicious spirits and shadow people were concentrated in that area. Tall stone quarry walls pressed towards us from one side of the trail while a sharp drop towards the river lined the other side. It definitely created a feeling of claustrophobia.

A tiny control building by the power plant's massive turbine housing was generously supplying us with one photo anomaly after another. One of the team would ask, "Does anyone here want to be seen?" A flood of strange lights

The Robert E. Lee Memorial Bridge shadows the portion of the island that once held Union prisoners.

would appear in the digital images. We stayed there snapping photos for about thirty minutes until the activity faded away. This was the first time many of the investigators on the team had experienced photo anomalies that actually responded to their questions and provocations and none were disappointed.

After snapping hundreds of photos near the old power plant, we moved on to the spot where the boundary of the prison area was located, under the busy "General R. E. Lee Memorial Bridge." The first Lee Bridge was

built in the 1930s to connect Richmond at the north side of the James River to its sister city of Manchester on the south side. Manchester was eventually absorbed by Richmond and the old bridge was destroyed when its replacement was completed in 1988. The construction of both bridges was handled with no regard to the archeological disturbance it created and many important structural foundations and artifacts of the prison were lost.

I thought it was a little ironic that this tiny island was shadowed by the city's largest memorial to its beloved Confederate General nearly one and a half centuries after Union prisoners there were freed. Did that somehow contribute to the maliciousness of some of the island's spirits? Were the prisoners that never left the island alive still attempting to fight back or escape? I was hoping to leave Belle Isle that day with at least a few clues.

Near the prison boundary we found an overturned tree whose roots so graciously brought to the surface some remnants of the old rail line that ran across the eastern side of the island. According to diaries and letters of the prisoners on Belle Isle, the rail line was both loved and hated. The trains were a welcome sight because they brought much needed provisions and an occasional load of shoes or blankets, though they were taken by the Confederate guards more often than not. Due to the exhaustion of the men and

the powerful rapids of the James River, the rail line was thought to be the only means of escaping the island. Many prisoners were shot and killed during their attempts at freedom there. Catching a rare glimpse of the railway's remains was a solemn event and the group was very quiet while reflecting on this discovery.

The Nailery

We continued towards the pedestrian bridge on the north side of the island and stopped to collect more photos at the ruins of the nineteenth-century nail factory building and its storage sheds. Slaves provided a substantial portion of the labor for the production of nails and other items made there from pig iron brought in on the adjacent railway.

Conditions at the factory were no doubt harsh and physically demanding. The "Nailery" operated on Belle Isle for nearly seventy-five years, even through the Civil War years when workers shared the land with Union prisoners. We all noticed what appeared to be "moving" cold spots in the area and collected more photographs until the anomalies eventually dissipated like those at the power plant. We then made our way back to the bridge and crossed the river at sunset.

Though we didn't collect any photo or video evidence that day that I would consider irrefutable proof of spirits inhabiting the island, both

Ruins of the Nailery

investigative teams that day came away with enough unexplainable lights, streaks, and shadows in our footage to convince most skeptics. The strange feelings of dread that were reported by all members of the group during our walk through, while immeasurable, were also so commonly reported by other visitors to the island. I felt certain something paranormal was to blame.

Still, feeling the rush of adrenaline from the excursion, I sat down to review the audio data I collected during our hike. I didn't know what to expect, but I braced myself for anything negative that might want to make itself known. After combing through nearly two hours of audio, I found one short segment that I thought sounded like a deep whisper. Unfortunately, the sounds of the crew talking, camera motors whirring, and the crunch of our footsteps seemed to drown out all of the subtle background noises where EVPs are most often detected.

Alone

I decided to make a trip back to Belle Isle just two days after our initial investigation, to leave my voice recorder in a quiet spot for a while. I had a feeling that if I went looking for voices alone I had a good chance of finding them.

The island was empty with the exception of a small handful of rock climbers near the quarry pond near the western bank. The buzzing of insects, chirping of birds, and steady rush of water over the nearby rapids were the only sounds around the old cemetery area near the footbridge. I tucked my recorder just under the edge of a downed tree about fifty feet from the main trail and less than ten feet from the graveyard. It was out of sight to the casual observer and in an area that few would even dare to venture.

To be sure I wouldn't hinder the recording in any way, I decided to move to the other side of the island to get a few more photos of the power plant and Nailery ruins. I announced I was leaving the area and requested that anyone who wanted to talk to me could send me a message though the device I'd placed beside the fallen tree. I also announced that if there was anyone there who wanted my help, to try and let me know by speaking. I often feel when I make those kinds of statements as I start recording, that I'm only talking to myself. But at that moment on Belle Isle, I felt like I had a very attentive audience.

I hiked about one-third of a mile to the south bank and collected more photos of both the interior and exterior of the power plant's turbine building and the smaller control building beside it. Being back in that area with the heavy, negative air and strange shadows had all of my senses on full alert. I registered every snap of a twig, flap of a bird's wings, and whistle of the breeze coming over the rocks from the surrounding river.

I caught movement out of the corner of my eye several times while I was pulling the camera away from my face, and quickly scanned the area

to find the source. I was mostly concerned with *living* dangers, but the thought of angry spirits crossed my mind as well. I didn't find a source of the movement—not even a bird in flight or leaves falling from the trees.

After thoroughly spooking myself for about fifteen minutes, I hurried back to collect my voice recorder before heading home—I couldn't wait to hear the results of the day's brief but intense audio experiment.

I wasted no time and grabbed my headphones as soon as I put down my gear. It was quiet without the crew's voices and footsteps and I was able to really concentrate on the sounds of the island. I listened to myself crunch off down the gravel path and took in the rhythmic rush of the water for three or four minutes. Then I heard something that nearly made me drop my recorder—a man's voice, heavy and clear, asking, "Where are we?" I'd never heard anything so pronounced in all of my other recordings.

Belle Island as seen from the north bank of the James River.

The logical part of my mind tried to rationalize that it must have been someone near the graveyard on the island that was trying to get his bearings. I backtracked and tried to hear a bicycle or footsteps approach on the noisy path. Nothing. The voice seemed to come from out of thin air. I replayed it about ten times and could find no explanation for what I heard other than it must have been some kind of paranormal contact. Every hair on my arms and neck stood on end.

I listened to the remaining portion of the recording and found no other oddities and definitely no other voices like the one I had already noted. Who was this man on the audio track? Why didn't he understand where he was? I felt a deep sadness that I had not heard him when he asked …

I formed my own opinion about the haunts on Belle Island that day. I knew in my gut that I wouldn't have been told the dozens of first-hand accounts surrounding the island there if there wasn't a root of truth to them. All of my doubts about

the anomalies in the photos collected the previous week were lessened and I looked at all of them a little more closely. I continue to hear about experiences with shadow people there and mysterious lights in the woods at night, sometimes two or three stories a week. I have a strong suspicion that they will not be stopping any time soon.

Of all of the haunts I have visited in Richmond, none made me feel as much like an intruder on sacred ground as I did at Belle Isle. Although it is a well traveled city park and popular downtown getaway, I truly felt like I was a guest of the spirits and had quickly worn out my welcome.

Malvern Hill

Mother Nature welcomed my visit to the battlefield at Malvern Hill with September's first day of cool weather. It had been months since I'd seen a day without the heavy haze of Virginia humidity, and I was thrilled that it arrived when it did. The drive down the narrow and winding rural highway took me through dense pockets of pine forest and past rolling farmland to a crossroads about fifteen miles east of Richmond. I had been told of so many similar paranormal happenings on and around Malvern Hill that I decided it definitely deserved investigating. There were very few indicators that I had actually found the place I was looking for, but the lines of cannon perched atop a bluff were a dead giveaway.

I pulled off into a tiny parking lot and gathered my gear. Just opposite the pull-off was a strange-looking clearing with two chimneys standing inside of an old split rail fence. I'd accidentally found the ruin of the Methodist parsonage and the site of dozens of reports of apparitions seen by drivers at night. Rumors of CB and radio interference at this short stretch of road were many, so I decided this would be the best place to set up my trusty digital voice recorder while I headed off on the Park Service trail through the neighboring woods.

I started recording and gave my usual introduction about the weather conditions, how far I was from a road, and details of things in the surrounding area that were likely to make noise. Placing the tiny recorder out of sight, tucked into a recess in the fence, about twenty feet from one of the old chimneys, I then started through the woods towards the old artillery field.

The Battle

The brutal and bloody history of the area, as with any battlefield, must certainly play a major role in the amount of paranormal activity that surrounds it. This land had seen more than its share of tragedy.

The Battle of Glendale, also known by some historians as Frayser's Farm, and the Battle of Malvern Hill just a few miles farther south, were both fought in the same area that now makes up the Malvern Hill National Battlefield Park. These engagements were the last conflicts of the Seven Days Battles at the end of June, 1862.

Following a strenuous battle and defeat at Gaines Mill, the Union Army was making their retreat south towards the protection of their gun ships

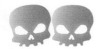

Ruins of the Methodist parsonage at Malvern Hill.

at the banks of the James River. Confederate generals ordered troops to prevent their Union counterparts from reaching the river by intercepting them and securing the area of what is still known today as Glendale.

The Confederates were hindered by disorganization, fatigue, and little or no provisions. Instead of one strong surge, their divisions arrived at different times and were poorly coordinated. Orders were misunderstood or not executed quickly enough, resulting in their giving the enemy the valuable opportunity to secure the highest ground in the area.

The Union set up a fresh battery of cannon behind a belt of trees at the bluff at Malvern Hill which was later called "an impregnable line of defense" by Confederate leaders. Confederates positioned their cannon as best they could to counter the Union's strategic line at their high point, and the battle soon turned into one of the largest field artillery duels of the entire war.

General Lee's army, then under the command of "Stonewall" Jackson, felt staggering losses over these two long days. The numbers of dead or missing Confederate soldiers totaled nearly 9,000. The Union army, though able to make their retreat, still felt the tragedy of having lost almost 7,000 soldiers in the two engagements. The few square miles around the old Charles City Crossroads were littered with bodies for weeks, and most were either buried in mass graves on the battlefield or in single graves where they had fallen. Many of the soldiers' remains were moved to cemeteries in 1866, but the final resting places of hundreds of men were unknown.

I descended the steep trail into the woods and made my way towards the creek at the bottom, following the same path through the trees that the Confederates had taken over a century ago when they discovered the Union Army's artillery line on the bluff. These historic woods had offered them the only screen of defense they had had on that terrifying day.

The woodland trail into the area Confederates used for cover was strangely quiet for a summer day.

The Strange Forest

I'm not sure if that knowledge was having an effect on my subconscious, but I noticed that the woods had become strangely quiet and I felt the sensation I was being watched almost as soon as I entered the tree line. My logical mind was telling me that it was only the birds and squirrels studying me, but I was also well aware of all the stories that came from that part of the forest.

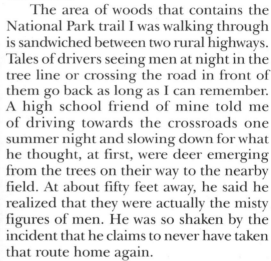

The area of woods that contains the National Park trail I was walking through is sandwiched between two rural highways. Tales of drivers seeing men at night in the tree line or crossing the road in front of them go back as long as I can remember. A high school friend of mine told me of driving towards the crossroads one summer night and slowing down for what he thought, at first, were deer emerging from the trees on their way to the nearby field. At about fifty feet away, he said he realized that they were actually the misty figures of men. He was so shaken by the incident that he claims to never have taken that route home again.

That same portion of the woods was also where Civil War re-enactor Tim Frederickson told me about an eerie cold breeze followed by an unexplained feeling of fear that swept over him during an encampment. Tim is especially sensitive to the emotions and physical pain that have been left by soldiers in what he calls *Psychic Impressions* around battlefields. He has, with uncanny accuracy, identified the sites of mass casualties, relying only on this sensitivity in places like Manassas, Cold Harbor, and others.

Shortly after he noticed the terror that seemed to blow in from nowhere at Malvern Hill, Tim recalls feeling an intense pain—as though he'd been shot. The pain was very

real and had him doubled over and immobilized in the woods. It lasted nearly an hour. He told me that he only later realized that he'd been standing at the Confederate front lines when the sensations came over him.

As with many other Virginia battlefields, the unmistakable sounds of cannon and rifle fire have been reported for miles around at all hours of the day and night. Rifle shots could possibly be attributed to hunters near the grounds, but area residents can provide no logical explanation for the booming cannon sounds.

The most commonly noted phenomena in the Malvern Hill area are the moving blue "cemetery lights" seen in the trees and, much like nearby Cold Harbor, the strange glowing mist that is said to settle over the battlefield. Both of these events are obviously best seen at night, but incidents of the lights in the forest have been reported in the daytime as well.

I snapped dozens of photos in the woods as I meandered my way through them. The sunlight was only trickling through the dense canopy of pine and oak here and it gave me high hopes of capturing one of the forest's spectral lights in one of my shots.

I took more photographs near the sunken gravesites of several exhumed Confederate soldiers and noted that they lay just a few yards inside of the trees. Could this have some kind of connection with the sightings at the roadside? The hairs on my arms and neck stood on end as this question entered my thoughts. I was at the same spot Tim stood when he experienced the wave of fear and pain. I hurried out of the trees and across the highway where the lines of cannon sat, as if frozen in time, on the hills in the field.

The field seemed so much larger when I looked out towards the horizon to the east than I had originally thought. I had seen it from my car dozens of times, but

Exhumed Confederate gravesite.

everything looks a little dwarfed when you are passing by at forty-five miles per hour. I could just barely make out the roof of the big white farmhouse near the spot where I had parked over the edge of the crest.

Collecting photos as I went, I hiked through the Confederate offensive line and traveled parallel to what remained of a historic farm road that had once been heavily traveled. This was the field with so many reports of the

glowing mist. I wondered if the gentle hills on all sides of me could have contributed to a natural fog that rolled to the lowest point on the landscape. That would make sense, but the "glowing" I had no explanation for. I had seen a mist like that many times in the 1980s and 1990s while passing farmers' fields near Fort Harrison—just a few miles from here. I thought, then, it was simply fog, but changed my thinking when I noted the strange bluish cast the mist created one night when the moon was completely dark.

I eventually came to an interpretive historical marker in the field that pointed out the locations of a plantation house and several slave quarters that once stood there. From that marker I learned that these fertile acres had a sad history that went back nearly four hundred years.

As I read, I noticed again the feeling that I was being watched. I heard no sounds from the soybean field to my left or from the woods to my right, not even a single chirp of a bird—only the droning white noise created by cicadas. I quickly marched east and found the line of cannon marking the site of the Union defenses, took dozens of photos, and ventured back to the old parsonage ruins to collect my voice recorder.

I have been investigating remote haunts in central Virginia for many years and can honestly say that, with the exception of Belle Isle, I seldom feel uneasy at a site during the daylight hours. By the time I made it back to my car that sunny morning, I was officially spooked and my paranoia was getting the best of me. I felt a prickling of anticipation of what my photos and audio recording might contain and hurried home to review my evidence.

The Evidence

I looked at each photo from Malvern Hill with a scrutinizing eye. Though I found nothing visual, on the audio I heard myself announce that I was leaving the recorder and listened to my feet crunch away through the grass. About ninety seconds into the recording, I started to hear an unusual clanking. It was heavy and almost rhythmic. I figured it must have been some kind of metal flap moving in the breeze on one of the chimneys at the ruin where I had left the recording device. I didn't recall anything in the area being metal, only the bricks and

The field at Malvern Hill where a glowing blue mist has been reported.

terracotta of the structure and the wood fence. I double-checked my photos of the chimneys and could find no metal whatsoever.

I listened closely as the clanking continued for about two minutes. When it stopped, I could hear nothing but a very light wind and the symphony of Virginia's late summer insects. I recruited my husband to listen and give me his opinion on the strange sound. I noticed he kept replaying one short segment. Just before the clanking started—he'd heard a voice.

I had been long into the woods by that point on the recording but a light, feminine voice was there on the audio file. We tried many times to understand what the message was saying, but it was too soft and unclear. At about three minutes into the track, he noticed the first of several distant shouts. They were clearly a male voice. While I had heard nothing at all while on the trail, the shouts I heard on the recording stood out and should have been obvious to anyone hiking in the area.

Though I didn't see, hear, or experience any distinct paranormal phenomena *during* my visit to the battlefield at Malvern Hill, I can tell you that I felt like I was being intensely studied by something or someone unseen. An eerie feeling of fear and hopelessness hung in those historical woods and made the air uncomfortably heavy. Instead of answering any questions I had or providing conclusive evidence of a true haunt, the audio recording I made at the parsonage ruins only sparked my curiosity to study the field and its surroundings in greater depth.

Chimborazo Hospital

Atop a hill overlooking the James River in Richmond's historic Church Hill district is a small park known as Chimborazo. Legend has it that "Chimborazo Hill," as it is more formally known, was named for a volcano in Ecuador because of their similar appearance at a distance. The true origin of the area's unusual name is unknown.

In order to form an opinion about what could be causing the tremendous amount of paranormal activity reported there, I had to first take a look back at the history of the site.

The park, which spans one and a half city blocks, is the only remaining open area of what was occupied during the Civil War by Chimborazo Hospital. The forty acres of open field at the edge of the capital, natural spring, convenient access to the city's railways, nearby canal boat travel, and major roadways of the time made the site a logical choice for location of the Confederacy's main hospital. With hundreds of wounded pouring into the city each day, the hospital was a cornerstone of wartime Richmond.

Chimborazo Hospital began treating wounded soldiers in October, 1861. It was comprised of wood huts that housed forty men each. Together, these simple structures formed the hospital's eighty wards, making Chimborazo the largest military medical facility in the world during the 1860s, with a capacity of 3,200 patients. Over 76,000 patients were treated by the commandant, surgeon James B. McCaw, and his staff, during its four years in operation with a surprisingly low mortality rate for the time of less than twenty percent.

McCaw's revolutionary hospital was both highly acclaimed and highly ridiculed. The war obviously created a demand for doctors and nurses who were well trained and ready to deal with the gruesome injuries resulting from battle and the diseases that spread so quickly in the camps and trenches. With nearly every man serving in the army, women were called in to fill the void by assisting with simple medical procedures and the caring for recovering patients. This bold move was thought, at the time, to be an act of desperation as women had never assumed these roles in the past. The female nurses, though, were well regarded by the patients and other medical staff, and many even made use of their skills after the war by gaining employment in local hospitals.

A Ghostly Nurse and More...

The discovery of the important role of women at the former field hospital rang a bell in my mind. One of the most commonly reported paranormal events at Chimborazo was the sighting of a woman in a long dress and apron walking alone in the park alone at night.

Richmond is not a terribly unsafe city, but when one sees a woman alone in Chimborazo Park after dark, it raises some concern. When approached by neighbors fearing for her safety, and even Richmond police officers patrolling the area on a few occasions, the woman simply vanishes. Witnesses say she doesn't appear to be distraught or in search of anything, she just walks slowly along the area near the bluff's edge with a thoughtful expression on her face.

Could the influential role of the women at Chimborazo Hospital be related to this mysterious lady's ghostly presence? Was she so deeply distressed by the injuries and suffering she witnessed in the wards that she left an emotional imprint on the area? These were just a small portion of the questions I was hoping to answer with my investigation.

More digging into the history of Chimborazo lead me to the discovery that the hill was no stranger to pain even before the hospital was erected at its peak in the late nineteenth century. In 1656, two very powerful and

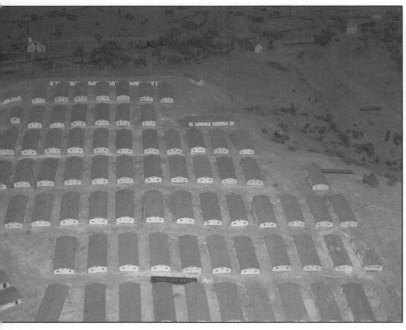

A model of Chimborazo Hospital is displayed at the National Park Service's Chimborazo Medical Museum.

competitive Native American tribes of central Virginia, the Siouan and the Algonquain, fought a desperate battle near the summit with the valuable piece of land near the James River as its prize.

Stories of the battle trickled down through generations of local Native Americans and some were even recorded in the exploration logs and diaries of the English settlers in the area at the time. The conflict earned the name "Battle of Bloody Run" because of the high number of dead and wounded on the hill that allegedly caused Chimborazo's spring and creek to run red with the blood of fallen warriors.

Tales of mysterious figures seen running near the southeastern edge of the hill and sightings of mysterious blue "cemetery lights" predate the construction of Chimborazo's famous hospital. Some witnesses claim to have seen men wearing furs and skins, hiding in the trees just below the bluff and along the steep drop to the old Bloody Run Creek bed. The disembodied shouts and war cries of Native Americans in the ravine there are still reported by early morning joggers in the park and by some of park's neighboring residents.

Historians have recently begun a heated debate over the location of the battle, some now claiming that it took place nearly twenty miles away, in Richmond's neighboring county of Hanover. Whether a tribal war was fought on Chimborazo Hill or not, historians all agree that the location was a very valuable one to the area's natives. Archeological evidence shows proof of their presence near the natural spring for several hundred years before the English made their claim to Richmond. While this added validity for me to the claims of spectral natives at Chimborazo, it raised more questions about the possible cause of such a haunt. Were these warriors fighting some kind of eternal battle, or were they spirits of the hill's former residents simply paying a visit to their earthly home? Again, more questions I hoped to answer.

The Medical Museum

At the western edge of Chimborazo Park is the Chimborazo Medical Museum operated by the National Park Service. Housed in a former Weather Service building, the museum features a macabre collection of Civil War era surgical implements, artifacts from the nearby Medical College of Virginia, and a remarkable scale model of Chimborazo Hospital and the surrounding area during the 1860s. I made my first of many visits to the museum in Richmond's oppressive August heat to meet Judy.

Judy, the attending ranger at the Chimborazo Medical Museum, let me know right away that she absolutely did not believe in ghosts. We

talked for a few minutes about the history of the former military hospital when the conversation drifted towards the paranormal activity reported on the hill. Ranger Judy shared a handful of her first-hand experiences and told me of hearing footsteps and voices in the museum building when she was there alone. An admitted skeptic, she agreed that these occurrences, while unexplained, should not be immediately blamed on spirits of the dead.

I have always been intrigued by supernatural events witnessed by those that deny the existence of the supernatural. I feel that their reports are worthy of a thorough investigation, because these skeptics seem much less likely to see what they expect to see or to let their imaginations take over. Judy's stories definitely fueled my curiosity and my eagerness to begin trying to capture some evidence of the supernatural in the area.

I took a handful of photos in the museum area of the building, the adjacent stairs, and the section partitioned off to house the tiny model of the hospital. I recorded a few minutes of audio in the exhibit room and a few more in the hall near the stairs. Having said my good-byes to Judy, I ventured out onto the grounds for more daytime shots of the area for my records. My plan was to return and drive the narrow park road after dark in hopes of photographing some light anomalies that were practically impossible to detect in the afternoon sunlight.

My nighttime drive of Chimborazo was made about a month after my initial visit to the museum. I waited for a clear night near the end of September that was free of Richmond's famous summer haze to eliminate as much atmospheric interference from the resulting photos as possible. The park was perfectly empty and quiet, except for the buzz of my car's engine, at only nine o'clock at night. I crept past the ring of benches at the center of the hill, snapping photos as I went, and moved on towards the edge of the bluff and where the most concentrated number of ghost sightings had been reported.

As empty as Chimborazo Park looked and as quiet as the grounds were, I still felt unseen eyes watching my every move and became extremely uneasy. I stopped the car, turned off the engine, and stepped out near the Powhatan Stone to attempt to record some EVPs.

The Powhatan Stone

The Powhatan Stone is a historical marker that has been surrounded with mystery and tales of supernatural guardians since its placement on the hill in the early twentieth century. The stone itself is said to have come from the site of the local Native American leader's seat of power, the area

just two miles southeast of Chimborazo, known today as Tree Hill Farm. Another rumor is that the huge hunk of granite was actually the marker of Powhatan's grave and had been moved to a more "convenient" place by city historians.

Either way, there is an undisputed connection of the stone to the influential leader that could be traced back to exploration records of the 1600s. The Powhatan Stone is probably the most controversial monument in all of Richmond purely because of its cloudy origins. I found myself wondering if the displacement of this supposedly sacred stone could have something to do with the reports of those Native American ghosts seen at the bluff, whoops and cries heard in the woods of the ravine, and the firefly-like "cemetery lights" seen flitting about.

I turned on my audio recorder and ran through my usual series of questions hoping to provoke a paranormal response. After about three minutes, I ended the recording and switched to taking some photos of the stone and the bluff surrounding it. I made no note of anything unusual in the area at the time—except for that pesky uneasy feeling that was sitting like a weight in my stomach—and returned to the car. I headed towards the eastern side of the hill—and the spooky round pavilion.

The Powhatan Stone is one of Richmond's most controversial and debated monuments.

Chimborazo's pavilion was erected long after the Civil War when the park was dedicated by the city in the early twentieth century. It is, however, no stranger to its own share of the Hill's ghost stories. The small but elegant structure is completely surrounded by windows on its circular frame, allowing those entertaining there to fully appreciate Chimborazo's beautiful view. In those windows, now covered with shades, area residents claim to have seen spectral faces and eerie glows.

The pavilion has had the interior lights go on and off at random times at night for several decades. Though old wiring could be at fault, the City of Richmond's Department of Parks and Recreation claims that the interior lights are always off unless the building is in use and that the exterior lights are kept on all night to discourage trespassers. They could provide no firm explanation as to why the lights turn themselves on and maintain that the building is secure from anyone gaining unauthorized entry.

I sat and watched the pavilion windows from a distance for what felt like hours. There were no faces or mysterious lights that I noticed. I took dozens of photos of the building until I was satisfied that I had collected enough data and headed home.

The Evidence

Combing through all of the images of Chimborazo took hours. The effort, though, was not fruitless. Two of the photos I took that evening contained a strange, misty glow and several unexplained points of light. These mysterious findings were in images that were part of two separate series of shots, both series taken in rapid succession. Of the eight to ten photos in each series, only one in each produced anomalous results.

I must admit that I was a little surprised to find anything suspicious at all in the photos from Chimborazo, but I was completely caught off guard with the locations where the images were captured. While my main focus during the investigation was the edge of the hill near the Powhatan Stone, I photographed as much of the park as possible for comparison. The first anomalies were in a shot taken near a small replica of the Statue of Liberty in the southwestern corner of the park. The second shot was taken of an open expanse of grass, used by locals as a play area for dogs, just north of the Pavilion. Two images turn out with the same mysterious shapes but taken minutes apart and in two non-suspect places? I couldn't just write that off as coincidence.

None of my audio recordings provided anything other than my own voice and cricket chirps, but the photos still had my thoughts swirling. Though I didn't see any mysterious lady, native warriors, or really anything else that could help be validate any of the stories surrounding Chimborazo,

A mist appeared on the right side of this photo taken near the southwestern boundary of the park.

Unexplained points of light appeared in only one of many photos taken near the park's play area for dogs.

the things I did capture were enough to prevent me from calling them all bunk.

Like any site rumored to be haunted, the only way I could come to a solid conclusion about the eerie hilltop would be to conduct a lengthy and controlled investigation. Unfortunately, such an investigation would be nearly impossible to manage in a heavily traveled public park. The old Weather Service building used by the Park Service has security cameras which could provide valuable data, but, sadly, none of them are keeping watch on Chimborazo's outer edges. Obviously, the Park Service is, and should be, more concerned with the well-being of their property than with keeping a lookout for spirits.

I'm not giving up hope, though, that someone will snap a picture at Chimborazo sooner or later that will stun the skeptics and believers alike. Until then, I urge you to visit this small patch of land and take a look for yourself at the views that made the spot such a sought after location. Take a few photos and listen carefully to your surroundings— you may just find yourself face to face with one of Richmond's most elusive spirits.

Gaines' Mill

Tucked away in the woods of rural Hanover County, just over a mile from the Cold Harbor Battlefield of 1864, is the site of a fierce Confederate charge against a strategic Union position known as Gaines' Mill. On June 27, 1862, the Union army was retreating from a defeat by A. P. Hill and his Confederate forces at nearby Beaver Dam Creek. Union General George McClellan and Lieutenant George Armstrong Custer decided to lead their troops to a high flat-topped knoll to defend against the gaining rebel forces that were hot on their heels.

The northern troops set up their artillery line on the clearing near the Watt House overlooking the natural boundary created by two steep banks that met at the narrow Boatswain's Creek about a quarter mile downhill. The Confederate forces had the Union army blocked on three sides and took heavy fire before sending in a surprising bayonet charge that allowed them to break through the enemy line. The Confederate charge was so effective that it forced the Union army to retreat yet again. The Union's field artillery gunners fled with such haste that they abandoned their cannon on the battlefield.

A Seldom Traveled Trail

The battlefield of Gaines' Mill is far enough off the beaten path of today's travelers that it is more a destination than a stop-off. Many of the locals that I talked to about nearby Cold Harbor had never even ventured up the tiny winding road to the old Watt Family Farm at the top of that historic hill. I had visited the site several times over the years to enjoy a hike on the National Park trails through the lush woodlands and to the scenic creek at foot of the ravine. I had never felt terribly uncomfortable anywhere near the battlefield, but I also had never felt that I was alone.

Many tales of strange sounds in the trees and sightings of spectral soldiers at Gaines' Mill trickled through to me quite often. One group of travelers from Massachusetts told me of their first-hand account with some of those sounds at the battlefield. The three men in their group of six decided to take the extension to the trail that led to the lookout point on the far side of the park, while the women returned to the parking area. About thirty minutes later, as dusk made its

approach, the ladies were standing around the cars talking about their trip, when the men came running between the fences down the field road, obviously very frightened.

Thinking that they must have encountered a snake or aggressive wildlife of some sort, the women were quite surprised when the men told them about being spooked by ghosts. The men had been standing at the lookout when they heard several nearby shouts, cries of pain, and then calls and moans of distress. They could see no one in the surrounding field or at the tree line and took off after concluding that the source was something paranormal. The whole experience lasted only about fifteen seconds.

Many visitors to the battlefield's beautiful hiking trails also claim to catch glimpses of men hiding behind trees, only to find no one there upon further inspection. One jogger told me of being startled by a man lying on the ground just off of the side of the trail near the memorial to fallen Alabama soldiers. She said she blinked and he was gone.

When I asked the rangers at the park about this, they told me it was not uncommon. Most of the sightings were in the area of several well-preserved rifle pits which allowed the soldiers to lie on their stomachs to fire their weapons with the surrounding earth and their low position providing some protection from enemy bullets.

Tim, the Richmond area Civil War re-enactor that so graciously offered to share so many interesting stories from overnight camps at area battlefields, told me of one of the most unusual accounts I'd ever heard from any haunted location. He had hiked down the park's main trail to the ravine where Boatswains Creek winds through the hills. Admiring a huge,

The long dirt road at Gaines' Mill that leads to the ridge on the park's boundary.

fallen "witness tree" that lay across the water, he heard a roaring that he described as similar to the sound of a huge flock of birds taking off from the canopy.

Primal fear took over as he tried to identify the cause of the noise and could find none. Tim, like the men from Massachusetts, opted then to run back to the open field near the parking lot.

Another commonly reported phenomenon at the battlefield of Gaines' Mill is the sighting of Union soldiers near the cannon on the ridge. The early morning joggers and the travelers at the park near sunset seem to have collected the most accounts. Some witnesses claim that the men looked

so real and solid that they at first thought they were historical interpreters there for a special reenactment—until the men disappeared. Others say that the figures were misty and their features were blurred, as though you were looking at them through dirty glass.

Collecting Data

According to the first-person experiences that had been submitted to me over the past few years, audible phenomena were relatively common at Civil War battlefields. Only Petersburg, however, had as many reports of visual phenomena as Gaines' Mill. I had to know what made these battlefields so distinct. The saturation of activity piqued my curiosity and I was eager to begin collecting data for myself.

I set out with my still camera and video equipment in hopes of capturing something paranormal on film. Just for the sake of science, I also grabbed my digital audio recorder to try and entice some EVPs near the lookout point where the tourists had been scared silly. I figured it couldn't hurt—I had been having some surprising results with it lately and was riding out the rush provided by those findings.

I made three different visits to Gaines' Mill to photograph and record any possible spirit activity in the dense woods leading downhill to Boatswain's Creek and in the sloping fields surrounding the Watt House at the center of the park.

My first was on an especially hot and humid day in late July. The moisture in the air was so oppressive that it made breathing difficult, but I felt a huge temperature difference as soon as I stepped through the tree line—inside the woods was cool and comfortable.

I made a slow and steady hike down the trail towards the creek, snapping images as I went. Pausing near a newly fallen tree, I switched on my voice recorder and asked a few questions. "Is there a spirit present that would like to communicate?" I waited about twenty seconds and asked, "What is your name? When did you die?"

The thought of what answers I might hear on the playback was chilling. I shook off the feeling and headed back down the trail.

The path took me to the creek where Tim had his eerie experience with the roaring sound and then back uphill into the section of the woods that saw the most vicious part of the battle. Rifle pits lined one side of the trail about halfway up the incline. I stopped again for another bit of audio recording, but this time I opted to keep quiet and just record the surroundings for about ten minutes.

The silence in the woods was unnerving. I couldn't detect a single bird chirp or rustle of leaves in the trees. There were no other tourists at the

park that day and the idea of sitting alone in that strangely silent forest triggered a gut instinct that nagged at me to get out of there. I packed up my gear, scaled the remaining part of the hill, and hiked back to my car.

Two days of carefully reviewing the photos and recordings from my visit to Gaines' Mill offered nothing conclusive. I found no lights, orbs, or mists in any of the images I shot. The closest thing to an anomaly I captured was a single blurry frame from a nondescript stretch of downhill trail.

The audio files took up most of the review time. I analyzed each with the computer, looking for even the faintest sound, but ended the search empty-handed. The frustration of a fruitless investigation at a place with so many first-person accounts of paranormal activity prompted me to make a return trip to the battlefield.

My second visit to Gaines' Mill was in early September. The weather had just turned from sweltering to tolerable and promised much more pleasant investigating conditions.

On the return trip I decided to skip the voice recorder and instead brought a HI-8 video camera in addition to my regular still camera. I also decided to shift the area of investigation away from the woods and to the grassy field near the Watt House and the ridgeline at the edge of the park where so many ghostly sounds had been reported.

I switched on the video camera and kept it recording while I walked the length of driveway around the Watt House, snapping a few still shots of the surroundings as I went. Progressing down the fence-lined dirt road

The Watt House sits at the center of the Gaines' Mill battlefield.

toward the ridge, I made slow and careful sweeps of the area near the woods with the video recorder. The entire park was as silent and spooky as it had been on my first visit and I didn't know if that was a good or bad thing. It felt as if a huge audience was watching my every move.

The ridge at the end of the road had a spectacular view. I could only assume that it must have been many times better during the war because the handful of trees that obstructed parts of the scene were all relatively young. I could clearly see farmland at least two or three miles away.

As I admired the view, I was startled by a sudden movement in the undergrowth just a few yards away. I spun in that direction, cameras at the ready, just in time to see a small brown rabbit dart out into the field. After taking a few moments to calm myself and to laugh off the surprise, I sat down at the ridge and faced the Watt House in the distance. The video camera was steadied on my knee and I panned the fields while listening intensely for any other sounds or movement. All was quiet. I recorded for about thirty minutes before calling it a day.

Reviewing the evidence from my second visit to Gaines' Mill took every bit as long as the first. Dozens of still photos revealed only the rolling landscape and peaceful setting. I moved on to the tedious chore of video analysis.

After examining the tape several times, I picked out two short segments from the portion recorded at the ridge that contained suspect sounds. Having exhausted my every resource to try and determine what the sounds were, I forwarded the video to a friend and recording engineer for his opinion. He used much more high-tech equipment and software than I even knew existed to pull apart the audio component of the recording in just minutes. With a trained ear, he manipulated the track several times, listened, and listened again.

His conclusion? I had either captured the sound of a sporadic breeze hitting the microphone at just the right angle or someone had been whispering only a few yards away. Both possibilities were startling. I recalled no wind at the battlefield that day—everything had been completely still and silent. I certainly had not heard any whispering onsite.

So what were these soft, breathy sounds? A fluke breeze that had blown by undetected at the time? I couldn't rule that out. A faint message from the other side? I couldn't really rule out that possibility, either. I was left with only the facts—I didn't know what had caused the sounds and I had no evidence to support the idea that it was anything paranormal.

The Watt House

A tiny wooden house, once belonging to the Watt family, sits surrounded by old oaks, magnolia, and black walnut trees at the top of the Gaines' Mill Battlefield. The exterior of the building has been remarkably preserved and the structure gives visitors to the area a sense of having stepped back in time. The interior boasts modern comforts like central heating and air conditioning and is currently the home of a Richmond area National Park Service employee.

The simple and unassuming home was the main farmhouse on the Watt's extensive orchard property. The family was well known for their bountiful apples, pears, and nuts that had been farmed on their many acres for generations. At one time, several sheds, storehouses, and slave cabins stood nearby, but today all that remains of the original farm are the house, one simple shed, and the Watt family's cemetery just to the south and west. The direct effects of the Civil War on the family and the war's personal impression on their property forever changed the Watt Farm.

The Watt House is currently the private residence of a park ranger.

The house has been modernized with heating and air conditioning for the comfort of the resident ranger and to help preserve the structure from Virginia's extreme seasonal climate changes.

In June, 1862 the Battle of Gaines Mill was fought just yards from the Watt's front door. Using the advantageous location of the Watt property at the top of the hill nearest Boatswain's Creek was the only hope that retreating Union forces had of holding back the Confederate attack. Cannon were set up in the family's fields overlooking the creek and, like most structures near battlefields, their house was seized for use as a field hospital to treat the severely wounded. They must have felt violated by having their home occupied like it was and they likely felt caught in the middle of the two conflicting armies.

A National Park Service film at the Chimborazo Medical Museum retells the personal accounts of the women at the Watt Farm having to bury all of the linens and blankets after the battle because they were hopelessly ruined by the wounds of the men treated there. The women complained that the floorboards of the old farmhouse were so saturated with blood that they remained purple no matter how many times they were scrubbed.

Mike Gorman, the attending ranger at Cold Harbor, told me of his experience helping to replace the carpet in the somewhat modernized Watt House several years ago. "I saw the blood stains with my own eyes," he said, "and they sent chills through to my bones. All kinds of strange things go on in that house."

The interior of the Watt House as photographed by the U.S. Government in 1957. *Library of Congress Call Number: HABS VA, 43-COLD, 2.*

One of the strange things I learned involved an electrician working several years ago to update part of the home's circuitry to support a new heating and air conditioning system. The story came to me second-hand from a trusted source, so I'm giving it the journalistic benefit of doubt. Allegedly, a ranger let the electrician into the house to work while he went on his regular patrols. When he returned later to make sure everything was secured after the work was done, the ranger found that the electrician had fled the house and left all of his gear behind.

When his employer was contacted about the incident, they were extremely apologetic and informed the Park Service that the man refused to go back into the Watt House. They offered to instead send someone else to complete the job and to retrieve the first man's tools. The electrician who ran off that morning supposedly still refuses to talk about any details of what scared him out of the house.

Several Park Service employees have shared the opinion that the Watt House could compete for one of Virginia's most haunted landmarks if they weren't afraid of the tiny residence being bombarded with trespassers and thrill seekers. Like the nearby Garthright House, the Watt Farm is currently occupied by a Richmond area Park Ranger and is not open to the public. Though the interior of the home is currently off-limits, I still hope to catch some proof of paranormal activity there.

I didn't let the Park Service's refusal stop me from trying to catch some proof of paranormal activity at the house, though.

The only real way to determine if the former residents or perhaps the soldiers that died in the Watt House are still around in spirit is to thoroughly investigate the building, both inside and out. I feel that something is there sending workmen running and making park rangers look over their shoulders. I hope to be granted permission to further my investigation soon, perhaps when the home is between tenants. Until then, I'll continue to collect and compare the Park Service's tales of hair-raising events witnessed in and around the solemn structure.

Cold Harbor

It was a hot and humid Saturday when I drove out to Hanover County. The tight and winding state highway took me about eight miles northeast of Richmond past rolling cornfields, clapboard farmhouses, and the leaning shells of abandoned service stations to a tiny five-way crossroads known as Cold Harbor. I followed the National Park Service signs and made my way to the battlefield—the cannons at the roadside let me know I was there.

Inside the tiny visitor center I met the park's ranger, Mike Gorman, and we went straight to the subject of ghosts. Mike had been assigned to the Cold Harbor Battlefield Park for ten years. He explained that, in that time, he has never heard or seen anything himself that one would consider paranormal, but he hears the same kinds of stories from visitors and the night patrol Rangers nearly every day. Occasionally, there is a report of some unusual event in the daytime, but he holds to the idea that the battlefield practically explodes with supernatural activity at night after the park is closed to the public.

In order to conduct a thorough investigation of the battlefield, I had to first examine the history of the area and determine which specific locations in the park I should target. Areas of greater casualties are a much more likely home to restless spirits.

The Battle of Cold Harbor is regarded by most Civil War historians as being the most lopsided engagement of the entire conflict. General U.S. Grant decided to move his men closer to Richmond and seize control of the valuable crossroads that would put the Confederate capitol in check. Union troops were utterly exhausted from their sixty-mile march from Northern Virginia to the edge of the huge area simply known as "The Wilderness." Because of the condition of his men, Grant held off an attack until the following day to allow time for rest.

Thanks to General R. E. Lee's network of intelligence, Confederate troops arrived at their destination ready to defend at nearly the same time as their foe. Despite low morale, hunger, and an ongoing shortage of supplies, Confederates used the few valuable hours while the Union was resting to dig massive trenches that would help them secure their position. This decision proved a valuable one and it had an enormous impact on the outcome of the battle.

The soldiers began exchanging fire in the cool morning hours of June 3, 1864. The fighting was intense and personal. Diary entries and letters to family from men in the field claim that the two armies were less than 100 yards from each other during some parts of the engagement. Charge after charge left the field littered with dead and wounded. Sharpshooters, some of the most feared and hated soldiers on both sides, hid in the trees and picked off men that tried to pull those still alive back behind their defensive lines. Three long and agonizing days of fear and suffering were

Cold Harbor's dense woodland is bordered by the open field where a ghostly fog is frequently reported.

brought to a temporary halt when General Lee gave the orders to cease fire and clear the fields of the dead and dying.

The Union army was devastated. They had nearly three times the casualties as their southern counterparts, estimated at over 16,000. Most of the men had the foresight to sew small patches of paper into their uniforms with their names and the means for reaching their next of kin in the event of their deaths. Lists of these names were made and counts of those who lost their lives were recorded as accurately as possible.

The number of dead was so high that the majority were interred where they fell. Occasional bursts of fighting occurred until June 12, 1864, when the few remaining Union troops were forced to withdraw. This defeat caused Grant to scrap his original plan for the siege of Richmond and spurred him to instead move his men towards Petersburg, about twenty miles south of the Confederate capitol.

General Grant said later about Cold Harbor, "I regret this assault more than any one I ever ordered."

Ghostly Occurrences

I thought sure that the reports of paranormal happenings at Cold Harbor had something to do with the strong emotions of the men who lost their lives there over a century ago. Locals and visitors alike claim to have felt the booms of artillery fire, smelled the distinct scent of burned gunpowder, heard shouts and cries from unseen men, the heavy clamor of horses hooves, and witnessed strange bluish lights and mists in the field and surrounding woods. Recounts of these occurrences are now part of Ranger Mike's daily routine in the park Visitor Center. He said that almost as many travelers come in hopes of experiencing one of these phenomena as come for the area's historical significance.

Though the number of paranormal reports coming from the site was dramatically high, I decided that I needed to see for myself if such incidents were truth or the product of urban legends. Cecily Garcia, a friend and fellow Richmond area paranormal researcher, arranged to have special permission granted to us by the National Park Service to conduct an intensive nighttime investigation at Cold Harbor. We put together a team of nine believers and skeptics, armed ourselves with cameras, night vision video equipment, EMF detectors, digital audio recorders, and even a portable cassette recorder that was easily as old as me, and secured a date for the outing.

Just two days before I ventured to the Cold Harbor Battlefield for our investigation, I was fortunate enough to meet two Civil War re-enactors at an artillery demonstration at Richmond's Fort Harrison. John and Tim were Union soldiers who were eager to participate in historical encampments and demonstrations at battlefields all over the country.

They both just happened to be very enthusiastic about some of the paranormal activity they experienced in many of these places—including Cold Harbor. Tim told me about one instance where he and a handful of other re-enactors were participating in a scene being filmed at Cold Harbor that was intended to portray a haunting at Gettysburg. The cameras were rolling as the actors loaded their cannon around dusk, when they noticed several men in uniform just inside the woods. Their excitement over these spectral soldiers was so strong that they couldn't focus on the scene and immediately shouted for the cameras to turn towards the trees in hopes of capturing the apparitions on film. The crew turned but missed their opportunity to photograph the entities by only fractions of a second.

Tim said that after they took a short break, the crew chief came to him and asked if the Park Service patrolled the grounds on horseback. She had been in the woods checking the light for their next shot when she claimed to see a man in dark clothes and a hat riding a horse near the Union trenches. Tim explained to her that she had just seen one of Cold Harbor's famous spirit residents.

The re-enactors are frequently allowed to camp overnight in true Civil War style at various battlefields for anniversary activities and other National Park Service special events. Tim and John were both overflowing with stories of strange sights and sounds at Cold Harbor that had moved even the most skeptical members of their group to rethink their position on the existence of spirits. Both men were very excited that an actual investigation was about to take place that could add validity to some of the things they had experienced during their overnight stays.

A story told to me by another re-enactor recounted how one night, after the men had bunked down to rest, they heard someone walking around the tents. Based on the clanking noises the person made with each step, they assumed it was someone carrying their gear and leaving camp early for some kind of emergency. They poked their heads out of the tents to see what was going on and found nothing out of the ordinary. All of their men were in their tents and accounted for and they saw no one in the wide open field near the camp. The men did discover, however, the strange sweet odor of jasmine hanging in the air that was detectible even over the smoke still swirling from their dying campfire.

The Investigation

I was geared up by my discussion with the soldiers at Fort Harrison just days before our investigation and couldn't wait to get into Cold Harbor with our cameras.

It was a calm, clear October night and the weather had just started to chill enough that we were in jackets by dark. I was struck by the fact that it was so cloudless and dry that you could make out the faint strip of the Milky Way after driving only a few miles away from the lights of

A bright blue light captured during our nighttime investigation at Cold Harbor.

Richmond's downtown. The moon was waning and it was huge and golden as it rose to the top of the sky. It was truly the perfect night for our trip to the spooky battlefield.

We arrived around ten pm and stopped in the paved area near the visitor center. Our agreement with the Park Service was to keep our vehicles there and stick to the paved roads and marked foot trails inside the woods. No problem. None of us wanted to get turned around in the wilderness and stumble into one of the site's many well-preserved earthworks, some were as deep as six feet, and a wrong step would surely result in a broken ankle or worse.

We met our law enforcement escort for the night, Barry Krieg, who was to accompany us everywhere we went. He was not a believer, but had an open mind and said he just had to see something for himself. I hoped we would have an experience before the night was over that would give him something to think about.

Ranger Mike had given me some tips that the greatest number of events reported supposedly took place between 1:00 A.M. and 2:00 A.M. That meant we had plenty of time to make it over to the ravine where the heaviest casualties occurred and set up some recording equipment. I was certain that if there were any spirits still lingering here at Cold Harbor that we would find them there, at the heart of the battlefield.

We drove through to the opposite side of the park and tucked our night vision camera in a safe spot behind a large stone monument overlooking the ravine. We had hoped to leave a second camera near the roadside parking area inside the Union trenches, but a strange battery failure rendered that piece of equipment useless. The battery had been fully charged and tested right before the night's outing. I was certainly disappointed, but thought this unexplained battery drain had to be a promising sign of an exciting evening.

After all of our video gear had been armed and positioned, we returned our vehicles to the parking lot and headed into the woods on foot. The tall canopy of oak and white pine caught nearly every bit of moonlight and enveloped us in a heavy darkness. Hiking about five hundred yards into the trees covering the Confederate trenches, we stopped to take our first series of photos. We moved on, crossed the roadway, and approached the southwestern edge of the main battlefield.

There was a peculiar tingle to the air and we decided to stop there for a while to snap more photos and collect some measurements of the electromagnetism in the area. We picked up only some tiny fluctuations on the EMF meters, but the light anomalies in our photos were abundant

to say the least. About ten minutes passed before the photos became fairly normal again and we packed up and moved ahead. That's where we first heard what we referred to as our "shadow."

Those of us towards the tail end of our line were hearing what sounded like a straggler from the group following about fifteen yards or so behind us on the path. A quick check ahead of our position showed that everyone was accounted for. Our ranger checked out the area with his night vision monocular and didn't see anyone or any animal that could be the cause of the sounds. The sense of a follower stuck with us for the remainder of our investigation. Were we being tracked by some kind of spectral scout?

We eventually followed the trail out of the woods and onto the edge of the large field at that borders the highway at the front of the park. We stopped and captured more photos and then had "quiet time" in hopes of recording some ghostly voices with our audio equipment. The break by the field was peaceful and relaxing, quite the opposite of what we had been feeling deep in the trees.

Our stop ended after about ten minutes and we hiked back into the woods and towards the ravine where our camera had been stashed. The tiny infrared emitters greeted us from several yards away and we took another recording break near the stone monument, a memorial to the soldiers of the 2nd Connecticut who were almost completely wiped out in the battle. A few minutes later and we were walking up the scenic drive and into the Union trenches.

The trenches on the Federal side of park were graceful and curved and rolled in long rows like the wake of a ship cutting through still water. This was a sharp contrast to the deep ditches in the Confederate area that appeared to lay straight and parallel. The road took us through these Union hills and to one of the parking areas overlooking the main battlefield, the same spot we had had the earlier battery failure. This is where we made our lengthiest stop of the night to collect more photos and audio recordings.

One of our group members, Tad Hill, was trying to talk to whatever may be around us that may be willing to communicate in hopes of capturing an EVP. A cold wind suddenly snaked its way out of the woods to where we were standing. The breeze was strong enough to blow my hair but, strangely, no leaves rustled and the trees and underbrush were silent. My scalp began to tingle and I felt the hairs on the back of my neck rise when another group member, Ron, asked, "Do you feel that? It's like static in the air."

I felt it, too, and nodded to him that I could tell something was going on. Tad continued talking and we kept our audio rolling when the smell

of sassafras wafted out of the trees and wrapped around us like a blanket. Several other group members experienced the scent, and all noted that it seemed to be lingering in one small specific area around Ron, Tad, and me. An uncontrollable trembling came over us, not the kind of trembling of fear, but … something else. Tad stepped back and snapped a photo of Ron and me when the shaking started and about thirty seconds later the air seemed to clear, and we could smell only the dry forest again.

We took a few minutes to collect ourselves and marched on towards the area of the battlefield where the Union charge was led over the trenches and into the open. The men were practically massacred there. The eerie cold breeze blew by us a couple of times carrying that odd sweet smell, but other than that, the area was quiet. No strange lights in our photos and nothing unusual to note. We walked on and into the opposite end of the Confederate trenches from our starting point of the night.

Dozens of photos taken during the investigation showed vivid orbs over the area of the Union Army's main charge.

As soon as we rounded the bend in the road that the park rangers call the Confederate Turnout, it felt as though we were walking through a cemetery. I had the odd sense of being where I shouldn't be and that I was disturbing someone. Many others in the group commented on having a similar feeling and we started snapping photos as we slowly made our way up the road.

Out of the woods and toward the main battlefield at our left, the most frigid breeze of the night suddenly came over us and dropped the temperature at least fifteen degrees. Just ahead on the road, we discovered that a thick fog about five feet high and twenty or so feet deep was following the cold breeze and settling like a weight on the battlefield. We had only a minute or so the take photos of the fog at a distance before it enveloped us and we couldn't see even three feet in any direction. Flashlights were useless and only made the visibility worse.

As suddenly as the fog had surrounded us, it moved on and was now isolated only on the battlefield. I took a quick glance at my watch—1:00 A.M. exactly. Remembering the tip that Ranger Mike had given me about the time of peak activity made my scalp tingle again as I looked out over this dense mist that appeared like a blanket of heavy snow lain over the field.

Orbs and a mist captured in the same photo taken near the Confederate turnout. The above photo taken immediately after the shot at right, showed nothing but empty woods.

Was the terrain here so remarkable and different from all of the surrounding farmland that the fog collected here naturally or were we witnessing something supernatural? We sat and observed the area for another half hour or so and packed up our gear for the night and headed out.

It took the team nearly a week to go through all of the evidence we collected during our night visit to Cold Harbor. Our audio

The mysterious fog at Cold Harbor rolled in and covered the battlefield in only a few minutes.

recordings were filled with strange sounds, but nothing that was clearly recognizable as a human voice or phantom gunshot. The night vision video offered no answers to the mystery of ghosts at the battlefield, but our cache of photos were so full of light anomalies and we had collectively experienced the peculiar chills and olfactory phenomena that we could not conclusively say that the area was *not* haunted.

The Rangers were quite surprised at the number of unexplainable

photographs we snapped that night and they even commented on how *maybe* there was some validity to all of the stories they had been told over the years. Our group was the first granted permission to conduct an official investigation at the park and we are fortunate to enough to have an open invitation to return once a year to collect more evidence, which we plan on accepting annually without hesitation.

Based on my personal experiences and those of my team members during our investigation, I can comfortably conclude that there is something truly special about Cold Harbor. We witnessed things so similar to the other reports of paranormal activity submitted from the battlefield that I'm confident that there is validity to the claim of a haunt. The evidence we collected in those few hours of investigating provided so many unexplainable phenomena that, even taking all personal feelings aside, the toughest of skeptics would have a hard time trying to refute.

In my opinion, this small crossroads battlefield in rural Virginia is surely the most haunted site of the Civil War aside from Gettysburg. In fifteen years of investigating and studying alleged haunts, I have never been presented with so many varied experiences and sensations at one location. I would

We were quickly engulfed in the thick mist.

suggest to anyone interested in seeking their own proof of ghosts to visit Cold Harbor—you'll likely take home more than just a collection of vacation photos.

The Garthright House

Just across the curving state highway from Cold Harbor National Battlefield Park sits a simple middle-class plantation house dating back to the late 1700s called the Garthright House. Due to losses of numerous pre-Civil War records, few details are known of the home's early years or of the identity of Garthright family members and others who were buried in the tiny cemetery right beside it.

The historical marker at the end of the gravel drive tells of the house being overtaken in 1864 by Union forces during the battle of Cold Harbor for use as a field hospital. Instead of being taken prisoner or turned out into the battle, the Garthright family was forced into the basement while surgeons above them worked frantically to save the hundreds of wounded brought there for care. The family later told of watching the horror of blood dripping between the floorboards to the basement where they were being kept.

It was not only Union army blood that soaked the floors of the home. After Grant's move from Cold Harbor to Petersburg, the Confederate surgeons moved to the house to treat their own men. Though the battle

The Garthright House is now a private residence for a park ranger.

[121]

lasted only days, this building was filled with weeks of death and dying, strong emotions, and the sorrows of war.

Just like in the fields across the road, the number of Union deaths was so high that the bodies were buried as quickly as possible and wherever there was room on the grounds. Many of the bodies were recovered in 1866 and moved to the National Cemetery, but nearly as many were left on the Garthright property because their resting places were unknown.

A Strange Visit

The Garthright House's dark and heavy history hung around me like a fog as I made my way up its narrow driveway. The building seemed a little mismatched by today's ideals with its lower left in brick and the rest in staggered wood siding. Its front was stark and flat with only the door's knocker as an ornament. The place definitely seemed solemn and lonely.

Much to my surprise, I found out only the week before my visit that the Park Service rents the former field hospital as a residence to one of its Rangers. Their belief is that an occupied property is far less likely a target for vandals and that a Ranger-in-Residence is good for the property's upkeep. That made perfect sense to me at the time, but then, seeing it with my own eyes, I wondered what on earth they had been thinking.

I've been told by a few residents of the subdivision just a few hundred yards from the Garthright House that they saw lights on in the home during the period when it was unoccupied. One of the law enforcement Rangers for the Cold Harbor area recounted a particularly amusing tale of a group of destructive squatters who were chased off by the mysterious knocks, bangs, and disembodied voices in the house nearly twenty years ago. Even though they were clearly trespassing and breaking at least a handful of other laws, the vandals were so disturbed by the events they experienced in the Garthright House that night, that they reported the strange sounds to a Ranger at the nearby visitor center the next morning.

Many local residents and visitors alike claim to have seen a young girl, around seven or eight years old, alone in the front yard of the Garthright House or just across the street at the gates of the Cold Harbor National Battlefield Cemetery. I was unable to find any records of a girl's death in or around the Garthright House, but area legend claims that she was the daughter of the cemetery's caretaker in the late 1880s, and fell to her death from one of the home's second story windows. Dozens of the reports tell of the girl's curious and playful nature and of her eagerness to interact with the living.

Though now closed to the public, my friend and local Civil War re-enactor, Tim, was able to tour the interior of the Garthright House several years ago when it was open during a Battle of Cold Harbor anniversary event. He told me that he had an uneasy feeling the entire time he was in the house and couldn't bring himself to descend the basement stairs.

I settled for a visit to the house for photos and a little audio collection from the public portion of the grounds. I parked off the side of the main loop, even though it didn't look like anyone would be coming by anytime soon, and got my equipment ready. I didn't know what I might find in the photos later, but I had a strong and nagging feeling that I was being watched. I started with some distant shots of the house and surrounding woods and moved to the closer angles as I made my way towards the family cemetery.

The cemetery was a simple rectangle, about twenty-five feet by seventy-five feet, enclosed by a short, mossy brick wall with an iron gate. What struck me as the most interesting was that there were no headstones or markers of any kind and that there was a complete lack of grass. It looked more like someone's empty garden than a graveyard. I snapped a few pictures and decided that it would be a good place to try and capture some ghostly voices with my audio recorder. I readied the device and started talking.

The family cemetery next to the Garthright House looked more like a garden than a graveyard.

I explained where I was, what the weather was like, and to expect to hear the occasional vehicle pass by on the state highway a few hundred yards away. I asked, "Is there anybody here who would like to communicate?" I heard no response but was hopeful to stir up some EVPs. "Is there anybody here still tied to this place?" Nothing. "I promise if you talk to me through this machine that I *will* be back." Still no audible response. I continued to record for about a ninety seconds, gave a warning that I was about to end the opportunity to be heard, and stopped the device. By this time I was getting a little suspicious of every tiny sound coming from the nearby woods and decided to head home.

I was barely in the house when I grabbed my oversize headphones and jacked them into the digital recorder. I landed on the couch and started listening for any faint voices or other mysterious sounds over the rattle of myself talking to no one. "Is there anybody here still tied to this place?" What was that? I backed it up and played it again—a distinct BOOM that sounded eerily like cannon fire! The sound was so real that I could even hear the echo of the explosion. But I had heard nothing out there at the Garthright House, so what was this?

I listened further. Another shot. I gave my warning that my recording was about to end and paused. Another shot! Every hair on my arms and neck was standing at full attention. I have to admit, I had my hopes up for hearing some disembodied voice up for a chat, but this was not a disappointment! I had to have a look at the photos.

The bright blue light in front of the wood separating the window panes was captured in only one photo.

I had snapped dozens of similar shots of the house and dozens more of the grounds. I scrolled though the images that seemed almost like a flipbook when one stood out from all the others. One picture of the house had a bright blue light near one of the lower right windows. I assumed it was a reflection of the sun glinting off of one of my car windows and went through all of the images again. I made my way back to the picture with the blue light when a thought occurred to me—I had only stood in two places to take all of those shots and nothing was reflecting in any of the others. I had been standing still for the picture before the suspect image as well as for the picture after it. I had simply snapped the shot, zoomed in a little, snapped, and snapped again.

I enlarged the area with what I thought was a reflection only to find that the blue light was not on the glass like I had assumed, but it was directly over the wood trim. My heart was pounding in my chest. I had no explanation for this photo anomaly. I filed the image away in my "jackpot" category and wrapped up for the day.

So is the Garthright House itself is haunted? Based on stories that I've been told by neighbors and Park Rangers in the area and the small amount of evidence I collected that day, I would say that there is some kind of paranormal activity on the *grounds* of the Garthright House. Given the home's history of violence and misery, it is easy to accept the theory that some sort of emotional "imprint" must have been left by the hundreds of frightened men that perished there.

As for the peculiar artillery booms in my audio recording, I cannot determine that they were an artifact of the Garthright property or of nearby Cold Harbor Battlefield. In either case, their source is unknown and the reason why they were inaudible on the grounds of the Garthright House is unexplained. I certainly feel that I came away with more than enough questionable data during my brief visit to convince myself that the rumors of ghosts in and around the old house are much more than just rumors.

PART THREE

PETERSBURG

Appomattox Manor

A short drive east of Petersburg, in the mostly industrial town of Hopewell, I visited a gorgeous home nestled in a historic neighborhood known as City Point. In my research before the trip, I discovered that the site had a long, rich history.

The eighteenth-century plantation known as Appomattox Manor was built on part of a land grant to the Eppes family from the King of England in 1635. It remained property of the Eppes until its transfer to the National Park Service in 1979. City Point was essential to U.S. Grant's plans for the siege of Petersburg, and eventually Richmond, because it allowed easy delivery of supplies to his forces via the waterways and the existing railroad.

The Park Service records claim that about 40 steamers, 75 sailing ships, and over 100 barges were delivering goods to Union forces along a half-mile wharf each day. Grant was prompted to set up his headquarters at Appomattox Plantation because of the easily accessible and well-stocked landing and the protection provided by gunboats in the adjacent river.

This plantation was different than any other I had visited along the James River. It was not a huge, overbearing structure that boasted wealth. Instead, it seemed to have grown naturally over time to accommodate the needs of the family it housed. The home was shaped like a "U" with the open side facing the convergence of the James and Appomattox Rivers. The setting was truly beautiful, and I could see why anyone would choose to settle their family there. Clad in simple white siding and topped with a red roof, the manor stood out majestically at a great distance.

I made my trip on a chilly Friday in early November. The winds coming off the rivers were crisp. Tightening my jacket around me, I grabbed my camera and hurried from the parking lot to the house at the end of the long, narrow walkway. I spotted a Park Ranger manicuring the enormous lawn on a surprisingly speedy mower and gave her a wave. I wasn't sure if she was the only one on duty, so instead of interrupting her mowing for entrance to the manor, I took my time exploring and photographing the grounds.

The kitchen and laundry building at Appomattox Manor.

On the western side of the house I found a collection of small shed-like buildings with locked doors and only one tiny window for light. I ventured into the open kitchen and laundry building, just steps from the manor house, and found several recreations of daily life from the 1860s. The kitchen was stocked with an array of cast iron pots, a hefty butcher's block table, and two pair of pantry cabinets at least eight feet tall. One wall was almost entirely taken up by a weathered brick hearth. The laundry side of the small building was empty except for a huge washtub and scrub board. There was another hearth here, but only about three quarters the size of its kitchen counterpart.

The majority of each room was roped off to prevent visitors from straying. In the back corner of the laundry room I noticed a dark staircase that ascended to the second story with a sharp turn. I couldn't help but feel like I was being watched from the shadows on the stairs. "Is there anyone here?" I asked and then snapped a few photos. Just out of curiosity, I knocked on the wall below the stairs and said, "Hello?" Nothing. All was quiet except for the occasional gust of wind and the lawnmower outside.

View of the railroad depot at City Point's wharf during the Union occupation of 1864. *LOC Reproduction Number: LC-DIG-ppmsca-08248.*

A well-preserved fireplace, once used for cooking, took up nearly one entire wall of the kitchen.

I left the tiny utility building and hiked around to what was formally the front of the house, the side that faced the water. The sun shone all the way through the back to the front of the upstairs windows and I could see no furniture or decoration. The first floor had a set of modern-style Venetian blinds hanging in the western wing and open, uncovered glass facing the river in the east. The East Wing, added to the manor in the 1840s, had a pair of tall windows in the parlor that were obviously very old and quite thick. The glass looked as rough and choppy as the water behind me churning in the high wind. I caught movement in one window from the corner of my eye, but

The north-facing facade of the manor.

had a difficult time deciding if it had just been a reflection on the antique glass or something else. I took another handful of photos, though, just in case.

Down the slope, east of the manor house, I found Grant's cabin. The marker at the site indicated that the cabin had been disassembled and moved to Pennsylvania, where it sat on display for over 100 years. The Park Service acquired the cabin, had it moved back to City Point, and reassembled it on the grounds at Appomattox Manor in the same spot it once stood. It was both fascinating and simple. I was struck that the tiny log structure whose windows I was peering into had once been a general's quarters. It was definitely several steps above a tent, but still raw and rustic.

My exploration led me farther east down the slope to a massive Union earthwork. The three-sided mound had once been the protective wall that shielded the soldiers who manned a beach gun. The massive cannon sat less than fifty yards from Grant's cabin. I couldn't imagine being awakened by the sound of artillery fire from something that size.

Near the earthworks, I discovered the remains of what looked like Victorian-era concrete curbing that probably once policed pea gravel in

The older East Wing of the home is rumored to be quite active paranormally.

Grant's cabin was reconstructed on the site in the late twentieth century.

the narrow pathway. The concrete remains made a straight line towards the manor house, passing under a huge arbor, heavy with sprawling Lady Banks Roses. Being an avid gardener myself, I snapped photo after photo of the elderly and abandoned garden. I felt a warming sense of comfort there despite the chilly wind.

The sound of the lawnmower buzzed on and I decided to make my way up to the manor's entrance to see if there was anyone else inside. Ann greeted me at the door before I could even ring the buzzer and welcomed me in. She escorted me to one of the oldest rooms of the home, near the center of the "U," and let me warm up while watching a Park Service film about the history of City Point and the plantation. After the film, she led me around the ground floor to take yet more photographs. I knew the house had a reputation for ghostly activity, but everything seemed nice and quiet, so I was reluctant to get my hopes up.

We stood in the old dining room studying a model of City Point during the 1860s when a loud roar of wind came through and made the widows whistle in their frames. I started to feel a little buzz in the air then, but credited it to the breeze.

Inside the Manor

Ann showed me to the East Wing. I looked into the parlor with the thick windows I had noticed outside. It was filled with furniture and other household items that had belonged to the Eppes, among them a huge oval mirror that was blackened at the edges with age. I caught movement in the mirror from the corner of my eye and turned to snap off a photo in hopes of capturing something in the image.

As soon as I pressed my shutter button, the camera reacted in a way that I've never experienced before. The lens retracted halfway, then fully extended as though I were zooming in on a subject, retracted all the way, and finally came to rest at its neutral point-and-shoot spot. Only the batteries weren't reacting. The screen had gone completely black and the camera had absolutely no power. I had just a half hour before loaded a brand new pair of lithium cells which should have been good for at least five hundred shots. I had only taken about one hundred photos so far that day.

I struggled with the camera more and it wouldn't revive. It wouldn't even retract its lens into the "off" position. That's when I asked Ranger Ann if she had had any personal experiences with ghosts in the manor.

"Oh, all the time," she replied. "We used to have visitors ring a bell at the door in the central hall instead of in the West Wing where you came in.

The dining room as photographed by the U.S. Government in 1976. *LOC Call Number: HABS VA, 75-HOPE, 1-6.*

The dining room today houses a museum display that includes the original door to Grant's cabin..

Most people would naturally try the knob before they noticed the bell, and we would hear the knob turning from our office in the other room. We used to hear that knob turning all the time when there was no one there."

She went on to tell me about the maintenance woman who saw a young boy in one of the second story windows as she was leaving one afternoon. Thinking that he was a child from the neighborhood who had snuck in and hidden somewhere, she went back in to find him and send him out before she locked up. After a long and laborious search, she never found any boy or any sign that one had actually been there. About a month after her report of the boy in the window, other reports started coming from tourists making claims of similar sightings.

I learned that many visitors had also told of seeing someone in the upstairs of the laundry and kitchen building. Thinking it was a vandal or trespasser, they'd reported the sighting to the Ranger on duty. Upon investigating, the rangers found no one in the building and nothing disturbed.

A Civil War Spectre

The most intriguing story of a ghost in the manor comes directly from the Civil War. Legend has it that while the Epps family still had possession of their home, a nurse took pity on a severely injured Union soldier and sneaked him into the basement of the house to tend his wounds. She treated him there for days.

The kind nurse caught word of a coming inspection by the Confederate Army and hid her patient inside of a tiny room walled off from the rest of the manor's basement. She concealed the door but apparently did not have time to cover all of the soldier's belongings. Confederates found evidence that the man had been receiving medical attention and arrested the nurse for aiding the enemy.

The former caretakers of the estate tell that the soldier died from his wounds after the woman's arrest. His ghost was supposedly heard scratching and banging on the basement wall and calling for help. They claim that human remains were found in a basement partition during repairs to the foundation in the 1950s.

I shared this little story with Ranger Ann in hopes of getting a firm "yes" or "no" about the supposed find in the basement. To my surprise, the Park Service could neither confirm nor deny any of the information.

I turned my attention towards the city's records concerning the plantation—if human remains were found, then certainly someone would have been notified, right? Again, my search was fruitless. Since I was unable to get that definite "no" from the Park Service, I decided to write this one up as an urban legend that still had a pretty strong whiff of truth.

The parlor as
photographed
by the U.S.
Government in
1976. LOC Call
Number: HABS VA,
75-HOPE, 1-7.

After listening to Ann's experiences in the house, I tried the camera once more and got nothing. I decided to make the long walk back to my car for a backup set of batteries. I was about twenty-five yards from the house when I switched the camera on again just out of curiosity. Much to my surprise, the camera came to life as reliably as it had every time I used it before the little incident inside the manor. Peeking into the viewfinder I discovered that the battery strength indicator showed that the cells were still nearly full. What? I was able to save the spare batteries for another adventure.

As I had suspected earlier that day, the camera batteries that I had assumed were dead were good for another few hundred shots. Can I rule out the possibility of a simple technical hiccup? I firmly believe that the timing of the failure was not chance. The feeling in the pit of my stomach was there, the tingle of electricity in the air, and the movement in the mirror I caught from the corner of my eye. My belief that the camera's odd actions were somehow related to the paranormal activity in the house was only strengthened when I left the building, tried the camera, and found it to be fine.

I shot another few dozen or so photos outdoors at Appomattox Manor before calling it a day. I couldn't wait to see how they turned out and felt sure that I'd captured some kind of anomaly in the house.

Reviewing my images, one photo from my trip that day offered something unexplainable. Photographed at the strange

The strange blur in the center of this photograph, taken in the former gardens of the manor, remains a mystery.

concrete-edged path near the rose arbor, there was an odd little "something" that seemed to be flying though the bottom portion of the frame.

Every shot that day was taken with a shutter speed suitable for sports and would have shown birds or insects as though they were frozen. This "something" was definitely in motion—very rapid motion. The image before the mysterious one had nothing of note and neither did the image immediately following it. The scale of the blurred object in comparison to the leaves near it showed it to be about the size of a baseball.

I was at a loss. I had other paranormal investigators take a look at the image and give me their feedback. Most had the same assumption

This is an enhancement of teh anomoly on the prior page.

that I had—it must be a bird or an insect. They quickly changed their minds after seeing the other images of perfectly still and clear birds in flight that I had captured on the manor's grounds that afternoon. The overwhelming response was, "I have no idea!" My daughter firmly believes that I accidentally photographed a fairy. I'll let you make that judgment for yourself.

My visit to Appomattox Manor was a memorable experience. Can I conclude that there is any validity to the home's most famous ghost story? Not exactly. I can't rule that it's simply a legend, either. I am confident that I experienced something paranormal while in the plantation house, something that I can't logically explain. I urge you to visit for yourself. Take a walk through this remarkable witness to history and trust your instincts when it comes to a phantom presence in the house, just remember to bring spare batteries.

The Crater

Of all of the Civil War battles fought in Virginia, the Battle of the Crater, on the eastern outskirts of Petersburg, sounds most like a Hollywood creation than a historical event. The Crater was the appropriately-named hole that resulted from a Union strike meant to blow Confederates out of their fort.

Pennsylvania miners dug a long, T-shaped tunnel under the defensive lines of the fort with the sloping terrain hiding their actions from their enemy. In just under a month, the tunnel was complete and loaded with four tons of black powder. When detonated, the explosion left a gaping wound in the earth 170 feet long, 60 feet wide, and 30 feet deep. Residents in the city of Petersburg, a few miles away, claim to have had dishes and other items break from the enormous impact of the blast.

Petersburg National Battlefield Park's Eastern Front now borders the Fort Lee Army Base. A family friend and retired Air Force officer, Charles, told me a peculiar story about one of his trips to Fort Lee

A Fort Lee soldier reported seeing a full-bodied apparition while jogging near Battery 8.

with his late wife. It was the middle of a cloudy afternoon when they were driving down Route 36, the highway that bisects the battlefield. Charles said he was rounding a curve, approaching one of the park road overpasses, when both he and his wife saw a man in dark clothes emerge on horseback from the woods on their right. When they slowed down to get a closer look, the man vanished without a trace. After a brief exchange of disbelief, they determined that they had seen what he referred to as "an image from the past."

A similar report of paranormal activity in the park was submitted to me by a Fort Lee soldier that had been there jogging early one summer evening. He claimed that he was on a trail near Battery 8, when he heard a rustle in the woods beside him. Thinking that he had startled an animal, he turned and saw a man in dirty, worn clothing looking back at him just a few yards away. "Sorry," the jogger said as he passed, thinking he'd surprised a homeless man sleeping in the park. His thoughts changed when he noticed the gear the man was carrying on his belt. He turned back just seconds after he ran by the man and found no one there.

A park ranger submitted an account that took place not far from Battery 8, at the picketed fort by the main crossroads in the trails. She was out in one of the park's all-terrain vehicles near sunset checking for late-day visitors. After passing the small log cabin-style sutler store, she spotted someone entering the reproduction soldiers' cabin a short distance away.

She stopped the ATV and called out to who she thought was a tourist to let them know the park was about to close for

The sutler store and soldiers' cabin where a park ranger also claims to have seen an apparition.

the day. No response. She called out again and waited. Still nothing. She walked over to the cabin, peeked inside, and found it empty. Confused and a little surprised by her findings, she surveyed the parking area and noticed that there were no cars.

She claimed she hadn't take her eyes off of the cabin from the moment she saw someone enter, until she went to the door herself, and she had not heard any footsteps anywhere in the area. There were no other exits from the tiny structure.

Were there spirits in the park that were replaying the past? If so, did they even know they were dead? The tales of apparitions that did not attempt to interact with the living were very intriguing to me and I hoped I might capture evidence of one on my visit to the battlefield.

A Visit to the Crater

The Eastern Front of Petersburg Battlefield Park is enormous. It took me hours to drive through its winding main road, making short stops at each battery to read the historic markers and photograph the sites. By

the time I neared the Crater, it was late afternoon and the sun was hanging barely above the last of autumn's foliage clinging to the trees.

I parked alongside a few other tourists and set out along a narrow path that led to the infamous mine shaft. Deer were nibbling on the browned grass in the surrounding fields and were completely ignoring my presence.

The entrance to the mine tunnel was in the bottom of a deep gully. A stairway led me down into a dugout lined with sandbags. This spooky recession made me invisible to the other park visitors. I was very aware of this isolation as I crept toward the opening of the tunnel for a closer look.

The mine had been closed off about twenty feet in because of frequent collapses of the antiquated framework. At the end of the open portion, the Park Service had installed a panel with an image of a Pennsylvania miner hard at work. It was much more interesting to see than a brick wall or barricade of boards, but it gave me an uneasy feeling to look down that tunnel and see a pair of cold, still eyes looking back.

I took more photos and climbed back out of the pit. I didn't really expect to find much in the way of the supernatural down here, so I headed uphill, paralleling the mine shaft, to the center of the battle's carnage—the Crater.

The entrance to the Union mine.

[149]

The first things I noticed when I reached the fenced area at the top of the hill were the gargantuan trees that dotted the edge of the Crater. Some had trunks larger than four feet across, which was an impressive size in this sandy-soiled part of Virginia. It was unusual to

see that the trees were so huge that they made the Crater seem small by comparison. The Crater of the present was just a tiny fraction of the Crater of 1865. Time and natural deposits had slowly filled the site of the explosion. The earth was healing a grisly man-made wound.

The historical markers showed surreal images of tourists visiting the Crater in 1866. Men and women dressed in their finest stood and marveled at the devastation around them. The macabre attraction even came complete with a strategically placed skull in the photo's foreground.

I photographed the area thoroughly, making note of many smaller depressions to the north and east of the largest. These holes were all that remained of Confederate counter-mines. The Rebels knew that something strange was going on behind enemy lines. Tunneling was suspected when chipping and digging sounds were reported. Though the Confederates never found the Union mine shaft, their attempts were only fifty or so feet off target. I couldn't imagine the underground skirmish that would have taken place if they had been successful.

Rounding the Crater, I captured images of the handful of memorial markers at the site that seemed to multiply every twenty years or so. When the other visitors had made their way back to their cars, I switched on my digital voice recorder and placed it on top of a massive granite monument. I stood silently for a while, collected the recorder, and headed for the parking lot.

Depressions in the hillside marked the location of the collapsing tunnel.

The Evidence

I took several days to analyze the photos and audio recordings from Petersburg's Eastern Front. Though I uncovered nothing conclusive,

I felt that the eerie sensations I experienced there were clues that something unseen was present. The tales that came from tourists, the retired military officer, the park ranger, and a number of soldiers from

The Crater now is only a fraction the size it was in the late nineteenth century.

Fort Lee were certainly chilling but, to me, their numbers alone spoke volumes. During the peak tourist season for the battlefield, May through July, accounts of suspected paranormal activity in Petersburg's Easter Front were flowing in at three or four per week.

The park is so large that the chances of catching a glimpse of an apparition or a phantom horseman are immeasurable. The narrow, winding roads create hiding places and shadows around every turn.

I enjoyed every moment on foot and in my car. The park was a lush forest retreat just on the edge of a gorgeous historic city and I would recommend it as a weekend trip for anyone with an interest in the outdoors. The clearly marked miles of trails provide an educational place to exercise while getting an up-close look at one of the most notorious battles of Civil War.

Who knows, you may just even get a chance to meet some of the men who lived that bit of history face-to-face.

Conclusion

Where did all of my findings from the battlefield investigations lead me? Am I closer to feeling that I've captured irrefutable proof of life after death? Yes. While I can't say that any singe piece of evidence I captured is like a "holy grail" of paranormal research, I experienced so many unexplainable things on this journey that I am comfortable with the conclusion that there is *something* supernatural occurring in these places. I've just had a tiny sampling of the big picture, though. To conduct a truly solid scientific study, one would have to collect data daily for a much longer period of time, perhaps even for years, and compare that data to some sort of control model. I am not such a tough skeptic.

The battlefields and other spots I chose to include in this book were selected because of the high numbers of unexplained experiences reported there. Some of the phenomena were reported directly to me or submitted through www.VirginiasMostHaunted.com. Others came "through the grapevine" of trusted friends and paranormal investigators and some were recorded by authors in the past.

Personally, I feel that the overwhelming number of first-person experiences reported from these places is a great indicator of spiritual activity. The case grows even stronger when you consider that for every one incident reported, there are likely several that are never shared. These experiences deserve the same attention one would give to tips submitted to police about open investigations. Both situations ultimately have the same goal—to solve a mystery. If any of these reports of paranormal activity holds the possibility of furthering research in the field or finding proof of survival of the human essence beyond death, should they be ignored? No, to do so would be a great injustice to all of those seeking answers for themselves.

I encourage you, curious reader, to venture out into the Wilderness, walk down the Sunken Road, cross the rapids of the James River to Belle Island, and see for yourself the other preserved grounds included here on my journey. Go with an open mind and you'll likely experience much more than a rich history lesson—you could come away with a ghostly tale of your own!

Guide to National Battlefields

Manassas National Battlefield
Phone: (703) 361-1339
Address: 12521 Lee Highway, Manassas, VA 20109

For maps of the area and detailed directions to the Henry Hill Visitor Center, visit:

> http://www.nps.gov/archive/mana/information/info.htm

Fredericksburg National Battlefield and National Cemetery
Phone: (540) 373-6122
Address: 1013 Lafayette Boulevard, Fredericksburg, VA 22401

For maps of the area and detailed directions to the Fredericksburg Battlefield Visitor Center or National Cemetery, visit:

> http://www.nps.gov/frsp/planyourvisit/directfred.htm

Chancellorsville National Battlefield
Phone: (540) 786-2880
Address: 9001 Plank Road, Spotsylvania, VA 22553

For maps of the area and detailed directions to the Chancellorsville Battlefield Visitor Center, visit:

> http://www.nps.gov/frsp/planyourvisit/directch.htm

Belle Isle (James River Park System)
Phone: (804) 646-8911
Address: 4301 Riverside Drive, Richmond, VA 23220

For maps of the area and detailed directions to the island, visit:

> http://www.jamesriverpark.org/general-location.htm

Malvern Hill National Battlefield
Phone: (804) 226-1981
Address: 8301 Willis Church Road, Richmond, VA 23231

For maps of the area and detailed directions to the Glendale/Malvern Hill Battlefield Visitor Center, visit:

> http://www.nps.gov/rich/planyourvisit/visitorcenters.htm

Chimborazo Medical Museum
Phone: (804) 226-1981
Address: 3215 East Broad Street, Richmond, VA 23223

For maps of the area and detailed directions to the Chimborazo Medical Museum at the site of the former field hospital, visit:

> http://www.nps.gov/rich/planyourvisit/visitorcenters.htm

Gaines' Mill National Battlefield
Phone: (804) 226-1981
Address: 5515 Anderson-Wright Drive, Mechanicsville, VA 23111

For maps of the area and detailed directions to the Gaines' Mill Battlefield and the Cold Harbor Battlefield Visitor Center, visit:

> http://www.nps.gov/rich/planyourvisit/visitorcenters.htm

Cold Harbor National Battlefield
Phone: (804) 226-1981
Address: 5515 Anderson-Wright Drive, Mechanicsville, VA 23111

For maps of the area and detailed directions to the Cold Harbor Battlefield Visitor Center, visit:

> http://www.nps.gov/rich/planyourvisit/visitorcenters.htm

The Garthright House
Phone: (804) 226-1981
Address: 5515 Anderson-Wright Drive, Mechanicsville, VA 23111

For maps of the area and detailed directions to the Cold Harbor Battlefield
Visitor Center, visit:

http://www.nps.gov/rich/planyourvisit/visitorcenters.htm

Appomattox Manor (Grant's Headquarters at City Point)
Phone: (804) 458-9504
Address: 1001 Pecan Avenue, Hopewell, VA 23860

For maps of the area and detailed directions to Appomattox Manor, visit:

http://www.nps.gov/pete/planyourvisit/directions.htm

Petersburg National Battlefield – Eastern Front
Phone: (804) 732-3531 ext. 200
Address: 5001 Siege Road, Petersburg, VA 23803

For maps of the area and detailed directions to the Eastern Front Visitor
Center, visit:

http://www.nps.gov/pete/planyourvisit/directions.htm

Bibliography

Bahr, Jeff. *Weird Virginia*. Sterling Publishing, New York, NY, 2007.

Barden, Thomas E. *Virginia Folk Legends*. University of Virginia Press, Charlottesville, VA, 1991.

Danelek, J. Allan. *The Case for Ghosts*. Llewellyn Publications, Woodbury, MN, 2006.

Davis, William C. *Death in the Trenches: Grant at Petersburg*. Time Life Books, Alexandria, VA, 1986.

Davis, William C. *The Illustrated Encyclopedia of the Civil War*. Salamander, London, England, 2001.

Furgurson, Ernest B. *Not War But Murder*. Vintage Books, New York, NY, 2001.

Greene, A. Wilson. *Civil War Petersburg: Confederate City in the Crucible of War*. University of Virginia Press, Charlottesville, VA, 2006.

Hennessy, John. *Return to Bull Run: the Campaign and Battle of Second Manassas*. Simon & Schuster, New York, NY, 1993.

LeShan, Lawrence L. *The World of the Paranormal: The Next Frontier*. Helios Press, New York, NY, 2004.

Maney, R. Wayne. *Marching to Cold Harbor: Victory and Failure*. White Mane Publishing, Shippensburg, PA, 1995.

O'Reilly, Francis Augustin. *The Fredericksburg Campaign: Winter War on the Rappahannock*. Louisiana State University Press, Baton Rouge, LA, 2003.

Stoeber, Michael F. *Critical Reflections of the Paranormal*. State University of New York Press, Albany, NY, 1996.

Taylor, L. B. Jr. *The Ghosts of Fredericksburg—and Nearby Environs*. L.B. Taylor, Williamsburg, VA, 1991.

Taylor, L. B. Jr. *The Ghosts of Richmond ...and Nearby Environs*. L.B. Taylor, Williamsburg, VA, 1995.

Taylor, L. B. Jr. *Civil War Ghosts of Virginia*. L. B. Taylor, Williamsburg, VA, 1995.

Zenzen, Joan M. *Battling for Manassas: the Fifty-Year Preservation Struggle at Manassas National Battlefield Park*. Pennsylvania State University Press, University Park, PA, 1998.